Astrology... on the *Move!*

Geographic, Travel and Locational Astrology

Other Books by Sasha Fenton

Sun Signs
Moon Signs
Rising Signs
The Planets
Understanding Astrology
Reading the Future
Astro guides: 1995 - 2000 (with Jonathan Dee)
Your Millennium Forecasts
2001 - Your complete Forecast Guide
(with Jonathan Dee)
Astrology for Living
The Moonsign Kit (with Jonathan Dee)
Forecasts 2002 (with Jonathan Dee)
Living Palmistry (with Malcolm Wright)
The Book of Palmistry
Fortune-Telling by Tarot Cards
Fortune-Telling by Tea Leaves
The Fortune Teller's Workbook
Tarot in Action!
SuperTarot
The Tarot
Body Reading
Tea Cup Reading
Dreams (with Jan Budkowski
Prophecy for Profit (with Jan Budkowski)
Feng Shui for the Home
Chinese Divinations
Star*Date*Oracle (with Jonathan Dee)
Spells
(for more, see www.zampub.com)

Astrology... on the *Move!*

~ Where on Earth should you be? ~

Sasha Fenton

ZAMBEZI PUBLISHING

First published in 1998
by Zambezi Publishing Ltd
P.O. Box 221 Plymouth
Devon PL2 2YJ
Fax: +44 (0)1752 350 453
Web: www.zampub.com
e-mail: info@zampub.com

Revised 2001
Copyright © Sasha Fenton 1998, 2001,2005

A catalogue record for this book is
available from the British Library

1998: ISBN 0 9533478-0-X
2001: ISBN 1 903065-16-X

Edited & typeset by Jan Budkowski
Cover design by Jan Budkowski © 1998, 2001
Printed and bound in Great Britain by:
Lightning Source UK Ltd
35798642

Dedication
to Robert Currey and Barry Street,
who have been there for us from the beginning...

Acknowledgements
Jan and I would like to extend our thanks to the following
friends and colleagues who have helped and encouraged us:

~ ~ ~

Jonathan Dee, Robert Currey, Barry Street, Martin Davis,
Sean Lovatt, Andy Pancholi, Roy Gillett, Anne Christie and
all those friends and clients who allowed us to use them as
guinea pigs while testing the theories in this book.

~ ~ ~

A word as well to our many friends in the British
Astrological and Psychic Society... thank you for believing
in our publishing business, before it got on the road at all.

Credits

Astro*Carto*Graphy and A*C*G: ® The Late Jim Lewis Trust, USA

Local Space: ™ Michael Erlewine, USA

Cover: A*C*G map courtesy of Eqinox, London

Solar Maps: ™ Astrolabe Inc. USA & Esoteric Technologies Pty Ltd, Australasia

Winstar: ™ Matrix Software, USA & UK

The maps in this book were reproduced using the Solar Maps software program

Contents

2

4

What is this book about?

Relocation astrology

The *movable* forms of astrology described in this book are useful if you are considering travelling anywhere or moving to a new location for any length of time, ranging from a short holiday to a lifetime - and everything else between. This form of astrology will help you to understand why it is easier for you to live, work, find love or simply relax in some places and extremely difficult to do so in others, even though on the face of it the locations may appear to be idyllic. Even if you do no more than keep in touch with family, friends and work associates who are at a distance, you will find the systems in this book terrifically useful.

Please don't be put off by the scientific sounding names that locational astrologers delight in using, because these names hide techniques that are not at all difficult to understand or to use. Even if you are totally clueless about astrology, you will soon be able to work out to which planet each of the colored lines on any commercially produced chart refers. Unfortunately, different products and different computer programs do use slightly different colors to represent the planets but there will be a key or a legend somewhere on your chart and this will help you to sort out which is which.

Astrology at home

While I was gathering information for this book I went to a couple of lectures given by American astrologers who were bringing these concepts to British astrologers and then, as my confidence in the subject developed, I gave a few talks myself. The audiences at these lectures were happy to hear about the travel and location aspects of this subject, but when I started showing them how they could analyze their homes and what was going on in them, the audiences took fire. The people feverishly noted down the ideas I told them about and they were obviously keen to try them out on their own homes. Later I added the concept of Feng Shui to this part of my talks and my audiences became even more fascinated.

This development has led me to include a household section to my book, and the beauty of the system is that it is not difficult to cope with. When we get into the technicalities, you will see that you have a choice of sending off for a Local Space chart which you would find extremely easy to use or making one up from your own natal chart. This will help you to work out exactly what is going on in your home and why, and what to do to make things better.

Who is this book for?

You may be an ordinary member of the public who has treated yourself to one of the excellent chart and report products sold by such firms as Equinox in the UK, Solar Maps or others in the USA and elsewhere. If so, this book will show you the theories behind the map charts that you have bought and it will enable to you to understand the meaning of all those colored lines and to interpret them for yourself. You will then have the choice of working out for *yourself* what is likely to happen to you if you decide to visit a particular place. Alternatively, you may prefer to return to your astrology supplier and order further reports. Either way this book will help you to understand the systems that are being used and also to get much more out of the interpretations that have been given. One thing is certain, and that is that the more you look into this subject the more fascinated you will become.

If you are a keen student of astrology but know little or nothing about the various forms of locational astrology, this book will make these techniques clear to you. Even if you are a skilled astrologer who is used to handling the usual forms of natal charting in addition to various kinds of predictive or other techniques, this book will serve as an introduction to a concept that may be new to you.

If you are thoroughly conversant with all the forms of astrology that are described in this book, or if you have an IQ that is off the Richter scale, then you may consider this book to be too basic for you but your students and/or clients would find it very useful.

Maps and software

Equinox supply elegant and attractive maps under the copyright name of Astro*Carto*Graphy and they supply a natal and/or relocated reports along with them. Armed with such a map and this book, you can get more out of this service than just what comes with the Equinox package. Another option is to contact a local astrologer, ask if he uses mapping software and ask him to run off maps for you. Nowadays Astro-maps tend to be known as ACG maps, and any decent astrologer should be able to supply you with these as well as Local Space maps. A skilled astrologer should also be able to produce Astro-geodetic charts for you. If all you ask for is the charts themselves with no interpretation work, the cost should be minimal. Discuss exactly what it is that you want before committing yourself to anything and always inquire about prices, including the cost of postage etc.

When I started working on this book in the mid 1990s there were only two companies that supplied map software in the UK and you will find advertisements for both of these in the back of this book. Nowadays there are a plenty of astrology outlets all around the world that supply map software either as a stand-alone item or as part of a generalized astrology package.

I am not aware of any Astro-geodetic program but this might now exist. Anyway, it is not difficult to set up this kind of chart by hand or to manipulate one by computer to give the geodetic Midheaven for a new location. If you don't know where to find a supplier in your part of the world, try visiting the www.microcycles.com site on the Internet, as this contains a vast range of astrological software.

The techniques described in this book

I have deliberately used the term *Astro-Maps* for the first of the techniques in this book. This name is becoming common now for this type of astrology and as such, it will be understood by any astrologer who is into geographic or travel astrology. In a moment, I shall explain why I have decided to use this name rather than one that might be a touch more familiar to some of you. Some of you will know this system simply as *'maps'*, this too being used on some of the professional astrology computer programs.

Local Space Maps

The chapters on *Local Space Maps* are primarily aimed at astrologers who have heard of this system and who would like to know how to use it. Some of you may even find it lurking somewhere on one of your computer astrology programs. There is nothing difficult about this kind of astrology and even non-astrologers can easily find their way around it, provided they can get their local astrologer to run off a *Local Space Map* chart for them.

The third part of the book covers *Astro-Geodetics* which, despite its off-putting name, is also an easy technique to use, but this definitely requires a measure of astrological skill. For instance, you need to produce a chart with an accurate Midheaven shown on it. The final section offers a guide to the relocation of all kinds of ordinary natal charts, progressed charts and solar return charts.

A final word for working astrologers

The moment you let your clients know that you can show them what their lives would be like when visiting other parts of the world, I can guarantee that they will want this service from you. If you business has been flagging a bit lately, consider adding at least one mapping program to your software collection and trying it out on a few charts so that you become comfortable with the system.

Where did the idea for Astro-Maps come from?

The true origins of the system that I call *Astro-Maps* are vague and they seem to have been originally used for *Mundane astrology*, which is the astrology of countries, cities, nations and politics. However, the man who developed the theories into a workable system for ordinary people was the late Jim Lewis. He coined the name *Astro-Carto-graphy* and the famous *Astro*Carto*Graphy®* logo. During Jim Lewis's lifetime and even since his death, this name has been known in astrological circles, but being registered has had the unfortunate effect of preventing it from spreading outwards into the wider astrological world. However, the original theories behind Mr. Lewis's system are not new or unique, and a good idea just cannot be kept in chains. Therefore, this book offers a simple explanation of the system, under the perfectly acceptable name of *Astro-Maps*.

In recent years, various astrology computer programmers have produced maps that allow astrologers to use this system, but with the exception of the Equinox and Matrix products, you will not see the term Astro*Carto*Graphy or its familiar acronym, A*C*G, on most of these maps. Both Equinox and Matrix have prior arrangements with the Jim Lewis Estate and can therefore use these terms. It has now become common for the Jim Lewis system to be known by the acronym ACG (without the stars between the letters), but as far as I know, the trademark situation has not changed and I don't want to tread on any toes, so I will stick to calling the system Astro-Maps in this book.

Who thought up the Local Space Maps theory?

This theory, like the previous one, is better known by the name *Local Space*. The chap who looked into the theories on *Local Space* and developed the computer programs to run them for popular use was Michael Erlewine of Grand Rapids, Michigan. The theories behind this form of astrology are not new, as they originally derived from the world of sailing and ocean navigation. The term '*Local Space*' does appear on a variety of computer programs and has turned up in a book by Steve Cozzi. However, again, in order to avoid inadvertently treading on anybody's toes and giving myself unwanted hassles, I will use the term *Local Space Maps* for this type of astrology, in this book.

And what about the remaining theories in this book?

Astro-Geodetics in its various forms has been around for years, I can remember working some of them out for myself way back in the 1960s. *Relocated charts* in various forms have been around for centuries.

A Brief Introduction to Astrology

If you have asked for an Astro-Map chart to be made up for yourself or for a friend, the chances are that you already understand a fair bit about astrology. However, for those of you whose knowledge is very vague, the following information should give you a very simple and basic overview of the subject.

The word *horoscope* means 'map of the hour' and an astrological birth chart shows in chart form where the planets were at the time of your birth. The signs that these planets occupy and such details as the *ascendant*, the *angles* and the *astrological houses*, alongside many other factors, show an astrologer exactly who you are and what you are like. The movement of the planets around the sky throughout your life show the trends and patterns unfolding. Fate sometimes exerts a powerful force upon us, but we do have free will, and our inner needs and feelings are as important as the force of destiny. The stars shouldn't be allowed to rule our lives, but they can be used in order to obtain guidance as to the best or worst times for taking certain kinds of action. It is, in the last resort, always up to the individual to 'go with the flow' or to choose to ignore the planetary signals. If you want to know more about *natal astrology* - the astrology of character and personality - and also *predictive astrology*, there are plenty of books, courses and even videos available for your information. Astrology of any kind is not hard to learn, and although the math is not difficult to grasp (just time-consuming), nowadays there are many inexpensive computer programs around that obviate the need for manual calculations. Even high street shops carry astrology programs for Windows now, and while these don't compare to a professional astrologer's program, they are a million miles better than having to work out and draw up a chart by hand.

Astrologers are used to dealing with *time*, and as far as the *timing* of events is concerned, astrology is an excellent form of divination but even the simplest form of astrology also deals with *place*. If you have ever visited an astrologer or if you have ordered a commercial report chart to be made up, you will have been asked for the time, date and *place* of your birth. If you move from one location to another, a good astrologer will *relocate* a *progressed chart* to take account of your new location.

Astro-Maps not only suggest what life will be like in a new location, but offer a fast and visual way of assessing *any place* in the world for its potential. This leaves all the choices up to you because only *you* can choose where you want to live or work. Even if you stay exactly where you are now but have family or other connections with people in different parts of the world, Astro-Maps will help you to see how these connections will work for you.

If you have ever ordered an Equinox A*C*G chart with an accompanying report, or a Solar Maps product, or indeed any such product, you may already have been asked to specify two or three locations that you are interested in. Your report will give a *natal* reading showing the astrological and geographic setup at the place of your birth, as well as any other locations that you have chosen to investigate. However, you may be interested in any number of locations, even if only to look into them for holiday possibilities. Whatever your interest in different locations around the world, this book will show you how to interpret for yourself all those fascinating brightly colored lines on any such chart.

How the Astro-Map system works

Make your own sunshine

Try the following experiment for yourself. Equip yourself with a globe if you have one, or a ball (a child's soccer or basket ball will do nicely). You will also need a torch. Stand the ball or globe on a shelf or a table and prop up the torch so that it shines on the surface of the globe. Then, depending upon the time of day, either turn out the lights in the room or close the curtains. Any large round object will do as long as you have a torch to shine on it. I remember on one occasion demonstrating this technique to a room full of psychics who had little if any astrological knowledge. The only thing that we had available to use for the demonstration was a large brown teapot. The method worked perfectly and the psychics grasped the concept with no trouble at all!

Shine your torch on the globe, somewhere close to the equator. The light from the torch will mimic the glow of the Sun. The brightest area will be like the spot on the earth where the Sun shines most strongly while the other side of the globe will be in darkness. The area where day breaks will be to the *left* of the sunlight and the encroaching night will be on the *right*. This is because the earth turns towards the right which, of course, is the east. The diagram overleaf demonstrates the point more clearly.

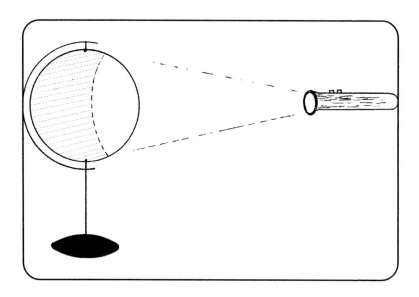

Simulating the light of the Sun

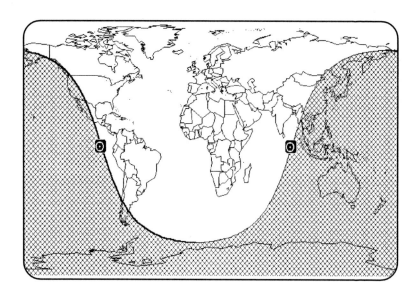

Chart showing day and night

The lower illustration on the opposite page is from the Solar Maps program, and it graphically shows the effect of light and darkness.

Now you have to do some mental aerobics so that you can understand the whole concept. By far the worst aspect of this whole subject is the confusing astrological terminology that goes along with it, and this problem stems from the fact that different companies use different terms for the exactly same thing!

Start your mental exercise by drawing an imaginary line, starting from the point where the Sun shines most brightly (i.e. Sun directly overhead), taking the line up north and over the globe, through the north pole and down the other side. Continue onwards by taking your line under the south pole and back up again so that it goes all the way around your globe vertically, just like a normal meridian line or 'great circle'.

Your starting point, the spot where the Sun shines most brightly, is called the MC, which is short for Medium Coeli (Latin for the top of the sky). The spot that is furthest away from the Sun, at the back of the globe, is called the IC (the bottom of the sky), which is short for Immum Coeli. The line to the *left* of the Sun where the light area (day) fades into the dark area (night) is called the *rise line* and the line to the *right* of the Sun, where it fades away into dark once again, is called the *set line*. Common sense will tell you that the area to the left (or the west) of the Sun is where day would be breaking on your globe, and the area to the right (or east) is where night is creeping over the face of the earth.

Here are some of the other names that you may come up against. As you will see, these terms mean exactly the same thing as the system that I have described above.

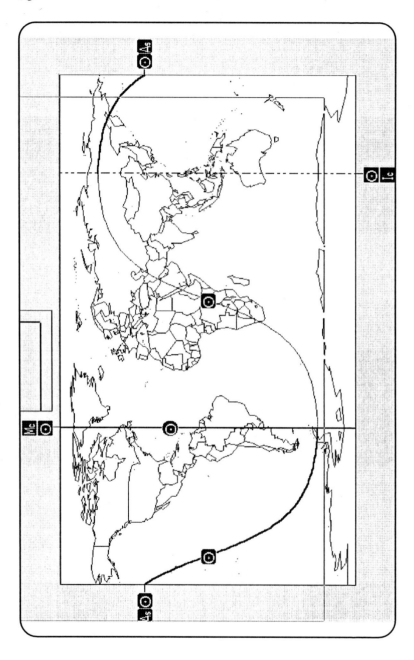

The Sun's MC, IC, Rise and Set lines

MC

The Medium Coeli, the Midheaven, the culminate line, the culmination, the upper culminate, the upper culmination.

IC

The Immum Coeli, the nadir, the lower-Midheaven, the anti-culminate, the anti-culmination, the lower culminate, the lower culmination.

The rise line

The ascendant - can be abbreviated to Asc. or As.

The set line

The descendant - can be abbreviated to Dsc. or Ds.

The energies of the planets

The areas around each of these lines is extremely powerful, it is hard to say how far to each side of any line its influence can be felt, although Jim Lewis suggested that the influences extended for about 300 miles (480 kilometers) on either side of a line. In amongst the very limited 'Jim Lewis' information that I could discover when I first began to study his **A*C*G** charts, there was mention of places to the east or west of certain lines being luckier / better / more powerful, etc. This puzzled me until recently, when the light suddenly dawned. However, this is not an easy topic to explain to a layman, but if you are already a pretty skilled astrologer, the next section will show you what this east / west business is all about. By the way, just to confuse things even more, some lines are so curved over that it is sometimes hard to work out what *is* east or west of any line, but if you are keen to understand this theory in detail, read the next section and look at the illustrations to see what is going on. If you are a layperson, you may want to jump over the next section until you know a bit more about astrology as a whole.

Further information for skilled astrologers

If you are a competent astrologer, you will know that the bottom half of a normal astrology chart represents those signs and houses that were in darkness at the time a person was born. If you can get your head around to the idea that the area on an Astro-Map chart that shows where the *Sun* was shining is exactly the same as the top half of an ordinary astrology chart, you will be on the way to understanding the next piece of information.

If the 'sunny' area on a chart represents the seventh to the twelfth houses, then it stands to reason that a city or a location that is to the east of the rise line (i.e. within the lighted zone), will be in the twelfth house. A location to the west of the sun's rise line (just outside the lighted zone), will be in the first house. This is because, when you think of it, the first house is *below the horizon* on an ordinary birth chart while the twelfth house is *above the horizon*. Similarly, if you look at the sun's set line, any location to the east of the line (within the dark zone), will be in the sixth house, while any location to the west of the line (in the lighted area) will be in the seventh house.

At this point, it won't take a super-brain to work out that any city or location immediately to the east of the sun's MC line will be in the ninth house and any that is immediately to the west of it will be in the tenth. Similarly, any location just to the east of the sun's IC line will be in the fourth house and any to just to the west of it will be in the third house.

This may in fact clear up some of the mystery of the inequality in house sizes that occur in some house systems, *especially when dealing with extreme northern or southern latitudes.* Even this is not the complete answer however, because all those ancient astronomers and astrologers who worked their house systems did so by a variety of different means.

If you have already passed this stage in your studies, you will soon work out for yourself how to divide up the world map into signs and houses. If you buy one of the advanced mapping packages, you will be able to enter these on to the charts for yourself.

The keys or 'legends' on charts

In addition to those that I have previously mentioned (MC. IC. Asc. As. Dsc. Ds. etc.), there are symbols or letters to indicate the various planets that these lines refer to. If you are getting a little lost here, just make a photocopy of the keys and keep them handy because all will become clear a little later in this book.

The symbols and the keys for the planets are as follows.

☉	SU	Sun
☽	MO	Moon
☿	ME	Mercury
♀	VE	Venus
♂	MA	Mars
♃	JU	Jupiter
♄	SA	Saturn
♅	UR	Uranus
♆	NE	Neptune
♇	PL	Pluto
☊		Moon's North Node
☋		Moon's South Node
⚷		Chiron

Maybe this is the time to invent codes for the nodes and Chiron, so how about NN for north node, SN for south node and CH for Chiron?

Finally...

The *ecliptic* is the path that the Sun appears to take around the earth. The Moon and all the planets are ranged on or close to the ecliptic. Your chart will probably show the wavy line of the ecliptic upon it but some computer programs offer you the choice of showing the ecliptic or of leaving it off. My advice to you is always to put the ecliptic on, as it really does help you to see what is going on.

Most map charts and programs will have some kind of symbol to show the MC of the Sun and of each planet and this may look like an 'O' with a cross through it or a small rectangle with a cross through it.

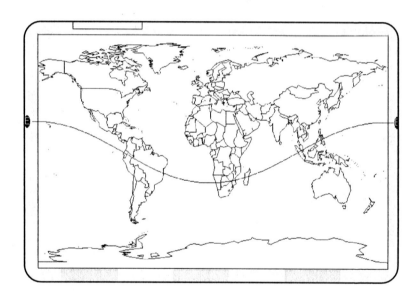

The Ecliptic

The Moon and the Planets

If you have performed the globe and torch experiment to represent the light of the Sun, you can now repeat it to demonstrate the light of the *Moon* on the surface of the earth.

We all know that the Moon doesn't actually generate any light itself but simply reflects the light of the Sun down to us on the earth. Moonlight is of course, much fainter than sunlight but the effects on a chart are just as strong, so your globe and torch experiment is just as valid for moonlight as it is for sunlight. Thus your Moon MC is where your torch shines brightest (i.e. where the Moon is directly overhead), your Moon IC is behind the earth where the torchlight can't reach at all, your Moon rise line is at the left hand edge of your torchlight and your Moon set line is at the right hand edge of the light.

So, now that you know how the system works for the Sun and the Moon, you must simply apply the same principle to all the other planets, even though they *cannot possibly* shine any kind of *visible* light onto the face of the earth. Thus, if you decide that your torch is showing you the way that Jupiter acts upon the face of the earth for you, you will have grasped the right idea.

Whatever planet you choose to think about while performing this experiment, the brightest spot will be at the *MC*, and the darkest spot on the back of the globe will be at the *IC* of that planet. The left hand (western) rim will be the *rise line* while the right hand (eastern) rim will be the *set line*.

Parans

Americans pronounce this word par*an* while Brits pronounce it *par*an - either is acceptable. A paran is the point where two or more lines cross and this is a very powerful point on your Astro-Map chart. The influence of a paran can be felt all around the line of *latitude* upon which it occurs, but obviously this influence will be far stronger around the area of the paran than thousands of miles away from it around the other side of the Earth.

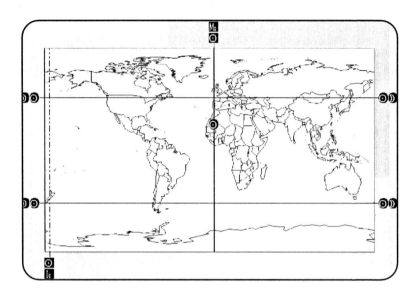

Paran and its line of influence

Overs and unders

(Hats and cups)

Looking at any Astro-Map chart, you will notice that sometimes the rise/set lines go up and across the MC line, with the planet's zenith shown on the ecliptic under the curving line, almost as though the planet was under a hat.

(The word zenith means a point vertical to the earth's surface; therefore, in this instance it refers to the spot where the planet is directly overhead).

At other times you will notice that the rise/set line travels under the planet's zenith across its MC line, almost as through the planet were floating in a cup.

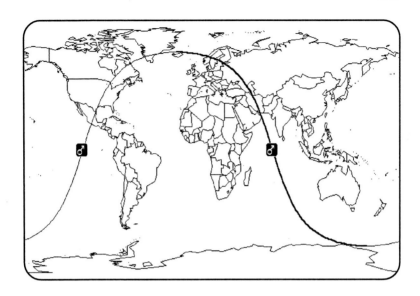

A "hat" shape

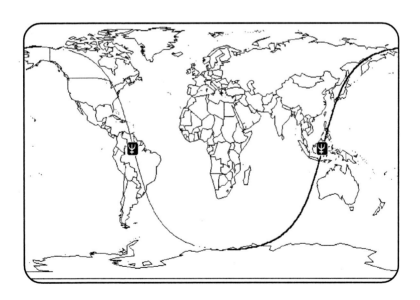

A "cup" shape

It doesn't matter which way up or down the rise/set lines are arranged on your chart, and if you have any difficulty in imagining the above exercises, just remember that they are interesting, but not essential, for you to understand the meaning of your Astro-Map chart. It is quite enough for you to see the lines on the chart and just to identify them; all the meanings of the lines are fully explained further on in this book.

Cyclo-Cartography

This term simply means the progression or the transits of any Astro-Map chart. Local Space Maps can also be changed to fit a new time or a new location. Your software menu will have these options on it. There is more about this later in this book.

Some Help for Beginners

As you go through this book, you will soon see how each planet works when it turns up on a rise, set, MC or IC line. However, the effects of any such move must be set against the basic nature of the person who does the moving, because a change of location will affect each subject differently, depending upon who they are in the first place. If you or any of your loved ones are relocating, the chances are that you know what type of person you or your close associates are, but you may want to look at this from an astrologer's point of view.

The moment that anybody delves into astrology, he or she very soon realizes that the planets, angles, astrological houses and many other factors on a birthchart go to make up the sum total of the person's personality. However, the kind of basic *Sun-sign* astrology that everybody understands can offer a kind of shorthand view of a person's nature. Some people are not like their Sun sign at all and in these cases, a visit to a good astrologer will soon show you why. However, for the majority who *do* have many of the normal characteristics of the sign that they are born under, the following guide will help you to see where you (or your friends) are coming from. The following list offers a little basic sun sign guidance, but if you need more information, there are plenty of books on the characteristics of the Sun signs.

Aries

This is a masculine, cardinal, fire sign, ruled by Mars. Ariens are energetic, enterprising, outgoing and competitive. The energies are expressed in an adventurous, impulsive, competitive 'I-want-it-now!' manner. These people want to be winners and high achievers and they have the courage to tackle almost anything. They have quick minds and often a good sense of humor, but they are rash and hot tempered. Ariens are big earners and big spenders and they lack patience with details. They can be charmingly childlike, but selfishness is their downfall and this can lead to problems in personal relationships.

Taurus

This is a feminine, fixed, earth sign that is ruled by Venus. Taureans are practical, patient, thorough, tenacious and reliable. They do things in a slow and patient manner, and they hate to be rushed. They are shrewd and they have common sense. These people are good with their hands and they are often very creative, musical and into making lasting or beautiful things. They can create and keep wealth and they don't like parting with money. They are good family members although stubborn, old-fashioned and sometimes boring.

Gemini

This is a masculine, mutable, air sign that is ruled by Mercury. These people are communicators and they will often work in jobs that involve travel and communications. They are quick and capable of doing many things at once. They operate by absorbing information, working on it and then passing it on to others. Geminis are good companions but some may be unreliable in long term relationships while others need a great deal of emotional and financial security. These subjects need variety in their lives and they are easily bored.

Cancer

This is a feminine, cardinal, water sign, ruled by the Moon. Decisions are taken as much by intuition as by logic, and these people need time to adapt to change as they move fairly slowly. Cancerians are emotional people but they sometimes don't pay enough attention to the feelings of others. These are shrewd business people who like to own a small enterprise of their own. Family is of paramount importance, along with emotional security. They don't trust others easily.

Leo

This is a masculine, fixed, fire sign, ruled by the Sun. Leos are proud, their standards are high and they can expect too much from themselves and/or other people. These people can be very glamorous and they like life to be fun. Leos can be arrogant, irritable and overbearing and they have to guard against snobbishness and bossy behavior, but they are generous, kind and they want their loved ones to be happy. They have less confidence inside than they display on the outside.

Virgo

This is a feminine, mutable, earth sign ruled by Mercury. Virgos are concerned with detail, careful diligent work, modesty and fussiness, but this doesn't always mean that they are especially neat or tidy. They are thorough, quick and efficient and they excel in any form of research work. They can be too independent, too particular and too awkward to make a success of close personal relationships, but they are usually valued in their jobs. They are happy to work but they also enjoy relaxing. These people have a terrific sense of humor and they make wonderful friends.

Libra

Libra is a masculine, cardinal, air sign, ruled by Venus. Libra is concerned with balance and fair play, but Librans can be unrealistic and unfair themselves. Outwardly pleasant and usually nice looking, these people can be hard to live with, mainly because they prefer to talk than to listen. They make good lawyers, counsellors and arbitrators, and they can sort other people's problems out even if they can't always deal with their own. Librans can be successful in business especially if they find a good partner to work with, they are artistic and clever but they can be lazy. Pleasant and kindly as friends, Librans can be too confrontational for personal relationships and despite looking cool, they can lack confidence.

Scorpio

This is a feminine, fixed, water sign, ruled by Pluto and Mars. Scorpios are all or nothing types who have strong opinions and fixed beliefs. They have great resilience and determination and they can hold on to people and things longer than is good for them. Tenacious and thorough, these people do a good job but they don't always have the interpersonal skills to be popular co-workers. Superficially charming, Scorpios can be hell to live with or to work for, although usually faithful and reliable in relationships and surprisingly fair - until they get into one of their paranoid moods. Scorpios don't like giving away secret or private information.

Sagittarius

This is a masculine, mutable, fire sign that is ruled by Jupiter. Optimistic and lucky, these people can drift through life having a great time while others pick up the bills. They are energetic, enthusiastic, sometimes sporty and quite hard working as long as their interest is maintained. If they lose interest in a job or a person, they move on, especially when the going gets rough. Highly intelligent, often wise and spiritual and normally extremely humorous, these people make great friends, as long as one doesn't need to rely on them.

Capricorn

This is a feminine, cardinal, earth sign, ruled by Saturn. These people are steady, reliable, modest and hard working. They are highly ambitious and apt to stay in a job, slowly working their way up to the top, bypassing others who appear to have far more promise. Quiet, thorough and unhurried, Capricorns can be too serious for their own good. However, they are extremely loyal to their families - especially their parents - and in relaxed moments they can exhibit a dry sense of humor. Capricorns can be fusspots.

Aquarius

This is a masculine, fixed, air sign, ruled by Uranus and Saturn. Aquarians are individuals and they are often 'different' from those who are around them. Independent, intelligent, ethical, humanitarian and sometimes plain awkward, they tend to do their own thing and live life their own way. These people can be too cool and detached in personal relationships and too overinvolved in political or social issues, and they don't always have their feet on the ground. Humorous and fun to be with, these folk make wonderful friends, but only good marriage partners if they can find someone who gives them space and who values them for their unusual natures.

Pisces

This is a feminine, mutable, water sign, ruled by Neptune and Jupiter. Pisceans may live for others, either by nursing, teaching and helping them or by sacrificing themselves to a needy relative or in some cases, a bullying relative. Pisceans are slow and rather dreamy but they are careful with money and often far better off than they look! Despite their loving nature, they often drift away from marriage partners, finding something or somebody more amusing to spend time on. Escapist tendencies sometimes lead to drink and drugs, but it is often art, music or mysticism that gives them the outlet that they need.

Helpful hints

You may have noticed that each sign is associated with one or two planets, and it would be worth bearing this in mind when you begin to read about the effects of moving to a place where a particular planetary line happens to fall. This is because this new planetary energy is bound to influence both your character and the events of your life in the new location. Therefore, if you move to a place where a planet that is already a strong feature in your chart becomes even more prominent, the effect of this planet will become even stronger. If you move to a location where a planet is weak on your own chart, this hidden influence will suddenly spring into prominence.

This concept is probably most interesting to those of you who have a fair amount of astrological knowledge because you will already know your Sun sign ruler, your chart ruler and which planets are prominent or weak in your chart. For a beginner, it is at least worth taking note of the planet that rules your Sun sign, as this would become extremely prominent if you moved to a location where this planet turned up on one of the angles on your *Astro-Map* chart.

For beginners

To give you an example, if you happen to be a Sagittarian and you move to Jupiter's rise line, you will become even more Sagittarian. If you are a Libran and you move to a place where Venus is on the MC, you will actively seek out a Libran career and Libran aims and ambitions in your life. If you are a Capricorn and you move to a location where Mars is rising, you will become much more forthright and less shy and if you are a Taurean and you move to location where Mercury is on your IC, you could suddenly discover a wealth of hidden energy that you use for a home-based business.

For astrologers

If you already have a planet close to an angle, the angle may change when you move but the planet will still be strong albeit that it begins to manifest its energies in a different manner. If you relocate to a place where your chart ruler becomes angular, you will become far more like your rising sign than you might previously have been. If you have a weak, retrograde, unaspected, detrimental or otherwise lousy planet in your chart and you move to a spot where this is angular - especially if this is the rise or MC line - it will improve this planet's energies greatly.

When I was living in Johannesburg, I met up with my Venus IC line. My own Venus is in its fall in Virgo, retrograde and succedent in the fifth house. Suddenly Venusian matters such as a lovely home, a terrific social life with music, food and drink shot into my life. I spent time buying clothes and cosmetics and changing my appearance for the better. Welcome Venus! Now that my new husband and I are back in the UK, we meet up with my Saturn rise line and his Mercury rise line and it is work, work and more work. Shame, isn't it! Maybe we will be able to go back to Jo'burg for a sexy, hedonistic holiday some day...

Interpreting your Astro-Map chart

If you are a non-astrologer and furthermore, one of those people to whom anything remotely scientific is total anathema, just look at the key color code or legend on your chart and follow the colored lines. Then look up the key to see which planetary line you are following - easy peazy, isn't it! Different types of charts may have slightly different colors for each of the planetary lines although some colors seem to be common to all the systems. An example of this is the Sun line which is always yellow.

An important point to remember

Obviously we all have a *natal chart* that is based on the date, time and place of our birth. The character that we are born with is always going to be with us. For example, if a person is sensitive and easily hurt, this won't change, or if a subject has artistic or musical talent, this won't suddenly disappear due to a change in location. However, we do change, adapt and progress throughout life and our environment is a very important factor in this. So all the suggested interpretations that are contained in this book can be considered as a kind of *overlay* or *modification* to the original chart due to the experiences both concrete and planetary that a change of place would bring.

A couple of examples of planetary lines

If you are familiar with astrology and conversant with the angles (Asc, Dsc, MC, IC), it won't be hard for you to realize that by moving to an area where the sun was rising at the time of your birth, you are temporarily giving yourself the effect of putting the sun on your ascendant. Your approach to life in such an area would thus become more sunny, Leonine, fun-loving, creative and outgoing. You may seek status and a good reputation at this spot and the chances are that you would find it. This would be an ideal place in which to have fun but you could be in danger of overdoing things and of falling ill with back or heart problems. In this place, you may become demanding, stubborn, arrogant and maybe even somewhat unfeeling towards others.

If you were to move to a place where Venus moves to your IC, it would be like overlaying your own birthchart with one that has Venus on the IC. Thus you could expect the area to be attractive and probably peaceful with a beautiful or valuable home, a pleasant social life and probably a nice looking garden. This would be a great retirement spot or holiday home and you could well find yourself singing, dancing, painting and maybe making love in such a spot, but it may be too laid back for ambitious goal seeking.

Angles rather than houses

In ordinary astrology, a chart is made up showing the four angles of ascendant, Midheaven, descendant and Immum Coeli but it also shows the twelve astrological houses. In *Astro-Maps,* we are going back to the earliest roots of astrology by concerning ourselves with only the four angles which are in this case expressed as the rise line, set line, MC line, IC line.

The Angles

If you are a newcomer to astrology, the following very brief outlines will help you to understand the following section of this book.

Consider the *rise line* to have a profound affect on your own personality and outlook, also on your approach to life and to the kind of things you want to be and to do. Changes would come here partly due to changes within your own heart and mind but also through being in a different environment.

The *set line* brings changes in relationships of all kinds and there may be very different types of people you will have around you in your new location to those whom you have previously been among. Differences in the way you relate will be partly caused by differences in your own attitude at the new location and partly by the outside circumstances that you find there. For example, working partnerships may come or go depending on the prevailing situation. Personal relationships that are already in existence may change radically and opportunities for new romance may occur — for better or for worse. You may want something different from partners, lovers and so on in a completely different environment.

The *MC* line will bring changes in your goals, aims, ambitions and it may bring a completely new kind of career. This could be brought about by the enlargement or shrinkage of opportunities in your new location but it may also reflect the changes that occur within yourself that come about as a result of your move. For example, if you leave a city environment in a cold wet country and move to a country area in a hot environment, your ideas of what you want to achieve and how you want to spend your working life could change out of all recognition. If nothing else, you will dress differently, eat different foods and live differently.

A new *IC* line will obviously change the way you live and the kind of home and domestic situation that you find yourself in, but a change of place can also bring changes in attitude. Home life is more deeply affected by changes of location than anything else, thus your way of life could be utterly different when on a new IC line. Certainly the way you feel about life in your new location will come more sharply into focus in your home than anywhere else. Once again, you may have to shop, cook, work, live and socialize in a completely different way in a new place.

A good example of this is my recent experience of living in Johannesburg. It is a beautiful city, but a terribly dangerous one to live and work in. Life in the drug-crazed Bronx has nothing on Jo'burg! I couldn't go out on my own much and when I went 'downtown' with my friend Vivien I sat in the passenger seat of her car with a loaded gun in my lap. Life for a woman in the wild west must have been fairly similar to that in modern-day Johannesburg! The countryside in South Africa is beautiful, our flat was large and comfortable and we have some really good friends in the area but life there is difficult and unpredictable. Living at that location brought Mercury and Venus to my IC, crossed by the Uranus rise line.

A vital last word

Remember that wherever you go, your *natal* chart still applies. This means that a change of lifestyle may bring up a hitherto dormant aspect of your personality and it may push others out of sight for a while, but *you are still you* and your own basic nature won't change all that much. Therefore, the interpretations in the next section must all be modified by your basic nature. For example, if you have a thrusting, aggressive nature, moving to an area where Mars is strong will serve to emphasise this, while moving to an area where Neptune and Venus are strong will soften your outlook and your lifestyle, but it won't turn you into a religious recluse or a wimp!

The Rise Line

Please bear in mind with all the lines that although these interpretations intentionally refer to those places where you move to, you can easily apply them to the place where you were born or where you have already lived for any length of time.

You should consider the *rise line* to have a profound effect on you personally, on your approach to life and to the kind of things you want to be and to do. Changes that occur here are partly due to changes within your own heart and mind but also through the effect being in a different environment. An example might be of a woman from a Muslim country where life is very restricted who relocates to an environment where opportunities for study, work and making personal choices come into effect. The reverse of this would be of a western woman visiting a place where women are not allowed any personal freedom.

The Sun rise line

Remember the rise line shows the way you act and think in your new location.

With the Sun's rise line in your new location, you would want everything to be just that little bit larger than life. If shyness has been an issue, it wouldn't be for much longer! On one hand, your self-esteem would rise to new heights but on the other hand, you would need more love and affection than ever. Your own attitude would be loving and affectionate towards your lover and also towards children, to animals or anyone else whom you consider to be worth loving. You would certainly begin to branch out and to make a good impression on others but you would have to guard against becoming vain, arrogant, childish or bossy. Your opinions would become stronger and you won't hesitate to express them. You may expect far too much from others, setting especially high standards for your lover, friends and work colleagues and becoming disappointed when these people turn out to have feet of clay. You won't be allowed to sit about too much here because external pressures, such as the need to generate more money or to reach an artistic or creative goal would goad you on to make more effort. However, any such endeavour would have a strong element of fun in it.

Children and young people would figure more strongly in your life, as would creativity. Indeed, your urge to create could also lead you to start a family of your own. You would be keen to set up a business of your own here and this may involve you in artistic pursuits or the creation of attractive goods such as jewelry or dress design. You would pay a lot of attention to your appearance, visiting the gym, the beauty salon and upmarket clothing shops as often as you can and you would become adept at finding high quality bargain goods here. You would be prepared to work hard, especially on any enterprise of your own but you would also be prone to lazy spells when all you want to do is to snooze in the Sun. This location could actually be a sunny one, but even if it is not especially so, the view from your window would allow you to see more of the sky and the Sun than you did before.

Gambling, dancing, singing or simply having fun would become much more important to you in this place. Success here brings an increase of status in the community, along with an increase in money and possessions. Once you have property and possessions of your own, you would try to hang on to them, taking as much of these goodies as you can if you eventually leave the area for good. The worst aspect of the

Sun rising is that you may become too self-centered and unwilling to give due consideration to the needs and feelings of others and you also may become intensely materialistic. However, your sense of humor and an increased generosity and affection towards others should help to offset any of the more overbearing aspects of the Sun's rise line. Another drawback is that you may just overdo everything.

You may become closer to your father or to father figures at this location. You may become more like your own father. It is possible that you would acquire a stepfather or mentor here and if so, this should work out well. If you are male, you may become a father, stepfather or grandfather on this line. Your health should be good here but your back and possibly your heart could become vulnerable to damage.

So to sum up. It can be fun living with the Sun rising, even if it is not always so great for those who have to put up with you! However, it would be best if this could be balanced by a more sober planet moving to one of your other angular lines. Better still, have a few lively holidays here and then go somewhere else later for a rest!

The Moon rise line

Remember the rise line shows the way you act and think in your new location.

Your emotions would be hard to live with on this line and you would certainly become far more aware of your feelings. You may change your outlook by becoming more private and secretive in some ways but at the same time oddly enough, you may have to deal with the general public more than was previously the case. The provision and presentation of food could become a feature of your life here, as could any other aspect of domestic life. A new property in this location would bring out your family-minded and domestic side to you even if you haven't been particularly interested in these things before. You would want to be loved and looked after here but you would also have a greater capacity to love and care for others. Whether you choose to look after people or to care for animals, your caring and loving side would be far more visible than it was before - but so would your moods! You may become weepy, crabby, demanding and difficult and you would also have to guard against becoming stingy or apt to jump down people's throats in an offensive manner.

You would become aware of your body and its needs at this location, and as long as you don't binge too much on comfort foods, your health would improve. Women with the moon in such a prominent position may fall prey to hormonal problems. It would be important for you to express anger at this location and not to push it down or 'swallow' it, or the result would be stomach problems at best or some kind of cancer at worst. Women may decide to become mothers here or you may suddenly take on someone else's child at this location. Either sex could acquire a stepmother or a female mentor and if this happens, it should work out well. Relationships with mother figures would become a strong feature in your life and such relationships may be marvellous, terrible or a mixture of both, but they would be *pervasive*. The past may become an issue here, either because your own past comes back to haunt you or because you would find past pain difficult to shake off. You may simply become interested in exploring the world of antiques or in genealogy here. This location may be close to rivers, lakes or the sea and it may also be quite a rainy one at times. Ships and boats may feature in your life here but even if they do not, you would be restless and inclined to take short journeys away from your home.

To sum up, you can feel as though you have *come home* when you move to a place on the moon's rise line but it can also bring you far too close to some uncomfortable emotions or bad feelings from your past. You may perform some kind of action-replay of past hurts and past disasters which would have a kind of cathartic or healing effect in the long run. The desire for a settled base in addition to change and travel would make you feel strange at times. To be honest this is not a bad place to settle in, there are plenty that are worse, but if emotions trouble you, then perhaps you ought to consider moving to a place that is less like to act as an emery board on your feelings.

The Mercury rise line

Remember the rise line shows the way you act and think in your new location.

The Roman god, Mercury, was the messenger of the gods and he was often sent to do Jupiter and Apollo's dirty work! Writing, talking and communicating of all kinds come into play here as this is where you would need to become a very good communicator. If you suffer from dyslexia, a stutter or any other form of communications problem, you would get the help you need at this location. You may change your job to include driving, business negotiations and liaising with others in a variety of ways; work that involves journalism or any other form of writing is a strong possibility. You may choose to work from home but you won't be isolated, because contact with people would become very important to you here. Even if you are a housewife with small children, committee work, contact with neighbors and getting out and about would become a part of your life. There may be disputes with neighbors at times but it is also likely that you would develop some very good relationships with those who live around you at this location. Relationships with siblings or other relatives of your own age would increase here. If there are no siblings, you could create a brother/sister type of relationship with a new friend.

You would become more talkative and possibly also flirtatious at this location and any shyness would gradually disappear. Depending upon your basic nature, you may find it hard to focus on one project, becoming interested in too many things at the same time and unable to plod through piles of boring work. However, if you take up sales work, driving, writing, computer, telephone work or any kind of career that offers plenty of variety, you would be able to concentrate enough to get through your day. Your health would improve and if you have been held back by an ailment this should ease, allowing you to get out and about more than before. Danger areas for health become the hands, arms, shoulders and also the upper respiratory tract. You may take up an interest in health matters yourself and it is possible that you may train as a therapist of some kind. Work would feature strongly in your life but you would become intensely interested in whatever you do and you should be able to make a success of yourself socially as well.

Some of you would find yourselves using tools at this location, perhaps by getting involved with do-it-yourself projects, while others would learn to drive for the first time. If you are already a competent driver you would change your driving style to fit the local conditions. The downside of Mercury's rise line is that you may become too talkative or unable to keep anything a secret. You would have to think hard before becoming too involved in the lives of those who are around you, especially if your new neighbors are involved in any kind of underhand or even criminal activity.

To sum up, a Mercury rise line is not a bad place to live in, but you could be too busy, too restless and maybe too unsettled at times. You would need to guard against concentrating so much on work that you forget to relax or to socialize. Your intellectual abilities would develop strongly here, as would your mathematical ability. If you do become interested in the health and well-being of others, you would also develop an interest in psychology and counselling at this spot.

If you choose to live on such a busy-busy rise line, it would be wise to select holiday destinations that offer you peace and quiet.

The Venus rise line

Remember the rise line shows the way you act and think in your new location.

Your looks would improve at this location, that's for sure! If you have let yourself go over the past few years, you would improve matters, possibly to the point where even a bit of surgical tucking, nipping and lifting may be on the cards. You would revamp your wardrobe and become far more stylish. All this takes money of course, but Venus would bring opportunities for financial advancement, possibly through marriage or working partnerships. With your improving looks and increasing self-confidence, you would find it easier to hold the interest of a lover or to attract a new one. You would certainly feel sexy here and you would develop the kind of sexual charisma that attracts well-heeled or good looking people to you. Your urge to find a soul-mate or a partner on this line could lead you into marriage. The problem is that the strongly romantic element of Venus can blind you to reality, leaving you to find out only later that you have misread the person with whom you fell in love. On the other hand, a relationship formed here could work out very well and it would be easy to keep a current romance alive.

Two rather unpleasant character traits may begin to appear, especially if these are already there buried under your present persona just waiting for an opportunity to break out. You could become lazy, greedy, selfish, demanding and unrealistic, or you might become lumpish and boring. Another - less than charming - trait is that of materialism gone wild, making you so money-minded that you forget everything else. To be honest, these are extreme examples which may well not occur.

Your artistic appreciation would increase here, so you could take up painting or learning to appreciate good music. You would become more conscious of your clothes and of the appearance of your home here. You would want to create beauty by working with your hands so gardening, craftwork, cordon-blue cooking could appeal. If you are into therapeutic or spiritual matters, you may be drawn to aromatherapy or color therapy either as a treatment for yourself or ultimately as something that you can do for others.

Venus's influence would make you sharply aware of injustices and you may join an organization that seeks to help those who are needy or exploited. You would certainly seek both justice for yourself and a sense of balance in your own life. However, surprisingly enough a Venus influence can lead to disputes, possibly in the course of trying to dispense justice and fairness to others or when trying to obtain this from them. Venus is associated with open enemies as well as open relationships, and this can lead to arguments and indeed, you may become extremely argumentative, even when there is nothing to fight about.

To sum up, most people would choose to live with the lovely planet Venus rising, but it can breed an unrealistic attitude and it can make it hard for you to achieve anything at all. Perhaps, it would be best if you have something more solid and settled on one of your other lines.

The Mars rise line

Remember the rise line shows the way you act and think in your new location.

Nothing and nobody would be able to restrict or repress you for long if you move to a location where Mars is rising. Your energy and drive would increase and so would your tendency to argue. If you move to this location along with a person who is accustomed to putting you down or putting you in your place, he or she would be in for a big surprise! If you have been ill, you would become stronger and fitter here, possibly taking up some form of exercise in order to become so. Your personality would be bigger and your manner more forthright than before. You would become far more self-orientated and inclined to consider your own needs, even if you have not been accustomed to doing so previously. Your concern for the needs of others come a lot further down the line than before and you could become quite a handful here!

You may now become involved in 'masculine' trades such as metalworking, engineering, car maintenance and anything else that brings you closer to machinery and tools. If for example, you are an artist, you could start to sculpt or make objects out of metal. You could take up a sport or become more athletic and you certainly would be more restless. If you are spiritually inclined, you could take up therapies that involve music, dance and movement or even iridology in this location (this is due to the connection between Mars and the eyes). Sitting around at home would lose its appeal as you stride around the countryside working and living in the fastest of fast lanes. Sex is an obvious area of interest with Mars rising, and sexual relationships could abound. If you have been the soul of faithfulness up to now, you may become very interested in experimenting with new bodies or new ways of making love at this location.

Relationships with men would increase and if you have lived and worked mainly among women until now, this would evaporate to some extent. You would need to curb your temper in order to avoid alienating others but oddly enough, your ability to charm others would also increase and you would use this to your advantage. Mars is really about power, so if aggression won't get you what you want, charm will, but either way you would get your own way much of the time. Don't expect others to be quite as delighted with your newly discovered ability to stand up for yourself as you would be. You would find courage here. You could fall in love on this spot and the chances are that your choice of lover would be a pretty thrusting, macho type of person of either gender. Sexual experiences are a strong probability and these would be exciting, powerful and emotionally overwhelming. Even if you subsequently leave this line for good, you would never forget the time you spent here!

Accidents and fevers are likely in this spot, so you need to curb any tendency to rush at things without watching what you are doing and you would need to force yourself to rest if you become ill. Unless you have a very 'laid back' type of natal chart, you would become impatient here. The experience of violence is a strong possibility on a Mars line, especially if Uranus and Pluto are also present at this location.

To sum up, a bit of Mars is a good thing but too much can be - well, just too much. If you have a couple of gentler planets on other lines, this would mitigate the Mars effect. If you have to be here for work purposes, try to make your home base somewhere else. If you *must* live here, take as many precautions as you can.

The Jupiter rise line

Remember the rise line shows the way you act and think in your new location.

Jupiter is a peculiar planet that has a better reputation than it deserves. In most books, Jupiter is described as the *great benefic,* or the planet that bestows luck, windfalls and blessings from on high. It might be just as well to remember that the ancient god, Jupiter (also known as Jove), had a habit of tossing thunderbolts down on to the heads of those who irritated him! Jupiter activity on a chart can and would destroy a situation in order to create the impetus to rebuild. Challenges may be set up here but the only thing to do with a challenge is to rise to it, so courage and the ability to think on one's feet would be rewarded. When those rewards come, they would do so quickly and in large measure.

Working life may expand terrifically here with the doors of opportunity opening up in wonderful ways and you may earn more money than ever before in this location. This situation increases the pressure upon you and it also raises the stakes.

We all feel unsure of our abilities when we are required to prove ourselves and you would probably need to do so at this location. Some people learn to enjoy country life as opposed to city life when Jupiter comes close, and an interest in animals could develop. You would make connections to people from different lands, different backgrounds and different religions and you may travel *more* once you are settled in this location than when you were elsewhere. You would experience a need for freedom on this line, so close personal relationships may be seen as an unnecessary tie. Restlessness and the need for change may make it hard for you to settle to anything at times.

Jupiter encourages study, so you may take up a form of training or education at this place and if you travel to this location specifically to study, you would enjoy the experience tremendously and you should succeed in your endeavors. Your belief systems may change, or alternatively, you would meet up with others who think and feel exactly as you do. You could take up an opportunity to study spiritual, religious or philosophical matters here. Your beliefs and philosophy would become much more important to you in this place and you won't be able to live in a way that goes against the grain of your personal morality.

Your health should be good here, but you should bear in mind that Jupiter's tendency to expansion may lead you to expand your waistline as well as your mental and physical horizons. Your liver and soft organs may need attention here. However, an increased interest in sports and games may help to offset any extra noshing or boozing that you indulge in at your new location. Your charm and popularity would increase and you would develop a sharp sense of humor, but you would have to guard against arrogance, overconfidence or pushy and opinionated behavior. The plethora of opportunities may encourage you to expand your horizons a little too far, thus leaving you exhausted and/or broke; however, a Jupiter location should be a lucky one with karmic benefits and maybe the odd windfall or two around the corner.

To sum up, living with Jupiter's rise line close by is exciting but it can make you overdo just about everything so the onus is on you to strike a balance.

The Saturn rise line

Remember the rise line shows the way you act and think in your new location.

Locational or geographic astrology is so new that very little has yet been written about it, but all that I have gleaned suggests that living with Saturn on any line is considered to be a recipe for hardship and misfortune. Well, I was *born* with Saturn on the ascendant and it comes into effect whenever I am living or working in or around London, which is most of the time! To be honest, my childhood and much of my subsequent life has not been easy, but the same can be said of a great many people whether they have a strong Saturnine influence or not. However, I have made tremendous achievements during my lifetime and I still have goals to fulfil. Without Saturn helping me to apply myself and to finish the things that I start, I can't see how any of this could happen. Many people dream of pulling off something great but they don't know how to translate those dreams into solid reality. Saturn's rise line brings dedication to details, hard work and 'stickability', especially when the going gets tough. In this location, you may take an interest in science or maths, while all kinds of exams can be passed here. Anything can be made concrete and lasting if you want it to. Some things (especially relationships), can last a little *too* long at this place.

Saturn confers a hardworking and independent attitude and this can and does lead to considerable achievements but it would be easier to win respect here than to win popularity contests. Oddly enough your feelings would be tender and deep and you can be badly wounded here, but you would struggle to hide your hurt from others. Shyness and inhibition may strike on this line and a cold outer attitude may simple be a defensive way of avoiding criticism, hurt or embarrassment. You happily take responsibility on this line, but you must guard against making a martyr of yourself. Learning to delegate and to trust others would be difficult but it is a lesson that you have to learn in this spot. Success can come on any planetary line, but with Saturn's rise line, the growth is slow but sure. Nothing happens overnight and the projects you choose would be long term ones that develop slowly.

Some of you could feel so overwhelmed by all the work or responsibility that is piled up on you so that you are tempted to retreat into apathy in order to avoid tackling anything at all. Chronic illness can occur, especially in connection with rheumatic or skin problems such as psoriasis. Tinnitus or other forms of hearing defect are also possible, but the potential for any ailment would depend upon your natal chart and also your state of mind at any one time. Illness may be a way of dodging some of the weighty responsibilities that threaten to land on you here.

There may be a connection to fathers or father figures on this line, or you may become a father yourself here. You may find a 'father-like' mentor or you could become someone else's father or mentor. Saturn is especially associated with doubt and fear, therefore fear of loss, poverty, illness or even fear of disgrace are all possibilities here. The experience of living with someone who frightens you is another possibility. A sense of balance would be needed and inner strength would be required to transform the problematical areas into lasting achievement and success. Eventual success and the financial benefit that this brings would help to increase your self-esteem. If you were born with Saturn rising it would be very hard for you to become truly confident, however successful you may appear to be to others. The jealousy that accompanies any success that you achieve can also damage your self-esteem, thus making this a confusing place in which to live. Confidence (or the lack of it), is a very Saturnian matter, and in this location confidence can evaporate, but it is by making the kind of solid achievement that can be seen, touched and understood by others, that turns the Saturnian drawback of low esteem into a pleasantly quiet inner strength that others recognize.

Finally, a couple of really good things about life on a Saturn line. If you would rather have a settled life than a changeable one, this is the place for you. It may be a little dull at times but it would be stable. Your common sense would come to the fore here, and you would develop an aptitude for detailed and thorough work of all kinds. Roots and structures go deep here, and anything that you construct in this place would last. Best of all, the friendships you forge here would run very deep and last for years.

To sum up, Saturn on any line is not easy but if you want to shine or to become rich, this would help you get there, albeit rather slowly. The hardships may be harder than usual here but the rewards of friendship and eventual self-esteem are worth having. However, it would be worth taking frequent breaks away from the area. The effects of this planet would be softened if there are other, kindlier planets lurking on or near any of your other lines.

The Uranus rise line

Remember the rise line shows the way you act and think in your new location.

Uranus is the 'break-out' planet and it destroys the rules that you may have lived by in the past. This is where you are faced with the truth about yourself and your lifestyle, and you may discover that you are not quite the person you always thought you were. Even the most retiring and respectable of folk can develop the capacity to shock others at this location. You may yearn for freedom, especially if you have been living under restraining conditions, or you may simply feel like kicking over the traces, even if there is little to be gained from this. The motivation for any of these actions is the need to be true to yourself and to express yourself freely as an individual.

You may take an interest in scientific or mathematical subjects here, and if you have never dealt with computers before, you would start to do so. Studying and learning would occupy some of your time here and you could take an interest in subjects that have never appealed to you or occurred to you to study before. Offbeat things would take your fancy because Uranus ensures that your mind would be open to many possibilities, even if some of them turn out to be bizarre. Your own behavior would become more individual, more eccentric maybe, as your mind seeks to discover new meanings for your life and new possibilities for freedom and expression. It is possible that you would study psychology and even become a counsellor at this location.

Relationships formed on this line happen *fast*, but they may not endure. Relationships that have become stale and restrictive suddenly end on this line - probably to the surprise of all those who know you. Similarly, you could throw up a long-standing career in order to take up something completely different. Sexual experiences would be exciting but there is no reason to suppose that these would be outlandish or peculiar, but on the other hand... Even if you are the most peaceful and retiring of personalities, you would lose your temper here and you could fall prey to unexpected emotions such as jealousy, hate and intense desire. Your health should be pretty good but sudden inflammations, headaches, unusual ailments or trouble with your ankles are possible.

You may become crazy, anarchistic, opinionated, stubborn or overbearing on this line and your ideas may become so far out that they defy reality, but at least you won't be boring! You would draw intelligent and interesting people to you at this spot, and your home would become a meeting place and/ or possibly even a teaching centre of some kind. Terrific friendships can be formed here and you would find people with whom you 'click', despite (or perhaps because of) the fact that they come from vastly different backgrounds to your own. Group activities would appeal to you and you may find yourself joining committees or becoming active in causes.

To sum up, Uranus is an exciting planet and a move to this line would certainly take you out of your rut, but this is an explosive and uncomfortable place to stay in for any length of time.

The Neptune rise line

Remember the rise line shows the way you act and think in your new location.

To be honest, I think this would be a great place for a holiday but probably not the easiest place to live and work in, unless you plan an artistic or creative career. Even then, it would help to have Saturn on one of your angles. Your imagination and artistic powers would flower on this line and you may take up an interest in photography and film-making, but it would be hard for you to turn your ideas into reality.

Religious conversion to any kind of religious or spiritual tradition is a strong likelihood here. You could become a recluse or a hermit who at some later date comes out of hiding to bring the world the 'message' that you have been given. Who knows, the world may even appreciate this! It would be hard for you to work, to get down to anything or to cope with material life in this spot and some form of escapism is a certainty. You may lapse into temporary insanity or zonk yourself out on drink, drugs or any other kind of unrealistic escapist behavior. You could become a slave to daytime television or you could simply find it impossible to get down to work here.

Falling in love is a prerequisite here! If you know you are due to spend time on such a line, be prepared to have at least one highly romantic affair. Don't expect to have a sense of responsibility or a clear head, and don't expect your choice of partner or the conduct of any love affair to make any sense to anyone but you and maybe your lover. When you leave this line and come back to your senses, you would feel that you had been under a spell - and perhaps you had! However, the experience would have been fun and you may well look back on this as the most exciting and fulfilling time of your life.

Neptune conceals, but strangely enough, it also reveals, so you may come to understand yourself or others more clearly here. This statement of mind goes against the grain of everything I have read about Neptune, but experience has shown me that this is true. Your intuition would develop strongly here, and this is probably the reason for the growth of insight and the clarity of thought. However, this still won't stop you from following daft causes, taking up with the 'wrong type of person' or generally playing havoc with your life. You would also need to avoid falling into the trap of living in a situation where you are asked to give or sacrifice too much for others.

To sum up, this line would bring an increase in artistic and spiritual development, but it is too hazy and unrealistic a place to live for long. Falling in love maybe wonderful but it may not last, or if it does, it might require too much sacrifice.

The Pluto rise line

Remember the rise line shows the way you act and think in your new location.

If you move to an area where Pluto is rising, your life won't necessary be easy but it would be interesting. Your feelings would run deeply here and there would be no room in your life for superficiality. However, you won't want to wear your heart on your sleeve, so you would go to a good deal of trouble to hide these deep or sensitive feelings from others. At best you would put on a bland expression but at worst you could develop a hard or a hostile manner that is designed to keep others in their place. This would be a pity because your need for close personal relationships would strengthen here. Your personality would become stronger and you could become a tremendous power for good. However, despite this added strength, you must guard against making a martyr of yourself to others. It would also be necessary for you to guard against manipulative or underhanded behavior at this location, and to ensure that you are as straight and honest with those who are close to you as is possible. Passions would be intense and there may be some really heated arguments. Sex could become an issue here and this too could be used as a weapon of a particularly underhanded or unpleasant kind.

Careers in an investigative field, such as journalism, health and medicine, or even police work may come your way here. You could find work in a hospital or maybe take up one of the many alternative therapies that abound these days. Helping people professionally would appeal to you, so counselling or psychotherapy might be on the cards. However, having too many friends crowding round you, wanting to take up your time and energy definitely would not. Financially, or in business, you could make some tremendous gains (or losses) here, and uniting with others in working partnerships or joint ventures would be very cost-effective and ultimately very remunerative. Some form of recycling or regeneration might appeal to you, and this could take a novel or offbeat shape. For example, you could start a campaign to save waste or to reclaim land, or you may turn scrap items into something artistic or useful. There is a fair chance that you would begin to hoard bits and pieces 'in case they come in handy some day', and your cupboards would soon begin to resemble a storeroom.

Your intuition would grow tremendously and if you take up an interest in psychic or spiritual matters while in this location, your awareness would become very acute. Spiritual healing should become especially interesting to you. If your life becomes unsettled here, this growing power of intuition would help you to choose the right path forward. There is a strong desire to unite with others here, but while your newfound paranoia may make you distrust them, your newfound intuition would show you whom you *can or should* trust and why.

You may find yourself living, as the Chinese proverb has it, 'in interesting times'. Political and social upheavals may affect you at this location and if Mars comes into play on any of your lines, the experience of riots or other violent events is possible. On a personal level, the need to transform yourself and your life would be strong and if you have been unhappy with your own personal development until this time, you can expect to take steps to improve things. This may require you to take up a course of training or education or to learn another language. You may give up a quiet life in retirement in order to go back to work, or you may give up work in order to retire. It is possible that you would start a family of your own here or you could leave one behind while you move on. If you are unhappy with yourself or your life, you would change it out of all recognition here. The change won't come as suddenly as it would if you had moved to a Uranian line, but a deep and vital transformation would occur. You would become aware of the big issues in life, those of birth, death, marriage and sex, and these events would touch you more here than in other places.

So, to sum up, a Pluto line is a great place to go if you need to change your existence but it may be too much of a good thing to remain on for more than a couple of years or so.

The Chiron rise line

Remember the rise line shows the way you act and think in your new location.

Chiron is not a planet, neither is it an asteroid or a planetoid. Chiron is a *Centaur*. A Centaur is a large piece of rock, the size of a large asteroid, that enters the solar system from outside and then can become locked into an orbit between some of the outer planets. Due to the astronomy of their orbits, they spend a good deal of time in some signs while whizzing through others. In Chiron's case, it takes about 52 years to go through all the signs of the zodiac. At the time of writing there are six of these Centaurs being investigated by astrologers, and there could be plenty more to come in future years. Chiron was discovered in 1977 and its effects are only now really being understood.

The original Chiron myth was that he was an ancient Greek god who lived in the form of a Centaur. Chiron taught martial arts, music and a whole host of other subjects that were deemed to be necessary in those days. He was also a skilled doctor, especially when it came to treating the inevitable wounds incurred by his gladiatorial students. Apparently, Chiron lived for many years (possibly centuries), working in this way, until he received a wound in his back leg from one of Hercules' misdirected arrows. The wound festered and Chiron's suffering became unbearable. He wanted to die but being immortal he could not do so. Eventually, he traded his immortality with Prometheus who had lost his, died and went on to become a star in the heavens.

Most astrologers have accentuated the teaching, healing and wounding aspect of Chiron. Those astrologers who don't know the Chiron story (and this seems to be the majority) call him the *wounded healer,* thus assuming that Chiron was busily teaching and healing others, despite being wounded or sick himself. However, according to the myth Chiron's long teaching and healing career came to an end shortly after he became ill. Either way, the general feeling about Chiron's position on a chart is that it shows the area where we teach, heal or help others. Also where we learn through suffering, then turning this experience to good use by passing on our knowledge to others.

Regardless of Chiron's effect on our characters at birth, any event that brings Chiron into play later in life seems to bring about a pretty violent change through illness or some other apparent disaster. The story that seems to emerge from the charts that I have studied is that those who have lived a life of unappreciated sacrifice for others - most often own their families - are brought to a point where they can no longer go on in the same way. In some cases, depression that is brought on by repressed anger and resentment erupts to change the status quo for ever. Often it is an accident or the discovery of a hitherto unsuspected ailment that brings the subject closely into focus with his or her situation. Chiron seems to put people in touch with their own mortality and their - previously unsuspected - mental or physical fragility, thus forcing them to change their outlook and their lifestyle.

Having said all that, maybe moving to a place where Chiron is rising could be a very cathartic thing, but I wouldn't want to live there!

The rise lines of the Moon's Nodes

Remember the rise line shows the way you act and think in your new location.

The nodes of the moon are the points where the moon's orbit crosses the ecliptic (the path of the Sun), first in a northerly direction and then two weeks later in a southerly one. Due to the differences in the calendar and the 27.5 day orbit of the moon, the nodes gradually travel backwards through the zodiac, albeit with frequent short forward lurches.

One of the theories of the nodes is that the south node represents one's past life and the north node represents the experiences and the karmic lessons to be learned during the current life. Therefore, if you were to move to a location that put the south node rising, there would be a familiar feeling about the situation, due to having been through similar experiences in a previous existence. You could find that the skills or knowledge that you need are already to hand, and it is possible that you could experience strong feelings of *deja vu,* or of having passed through this particular area in a previous life. This may be a bit speculative, but it is worth thinking about. The north node rising would, therefore, bring greater opportunities for the development of your soul and for karmic redemption, and the experiences that you would have here would be new to you in this life or in any other.

The notion of the nodes and karma come from Indian astrology, but before these were taken on board by western astrologers, some American astrologers decided that the nodes represented the prevailing social atmosphere. In this case, the north node represented philosophies or a way of life that blended easily with the current political and social atmosphere. The south node therefore, would suggest going against the political or social current. An example that I have given in a couple of my previous books is that of one person who wanted to open a health-food shop and another wishing to open a furriers. This example was written at a time when healthy eating, exercise gyms and so on were proliferating, while anybody dealing in fur fashions would have had paint thrown at them. Who knows, in ten year's time, fur may be in and health may be out, so whatever your goals are, just keep an eye on those nodes!

The nodes seem to have something beneficial to do with property matters, and probably family fortunes too. Fortunately, there doesn't seem to be much difference between the north or south node where this is concerned. Therefore if you are buying, selling, renting or improving property in an area where the nodes are rising, this should be a success - especially if you are doing this in some kind of partnership arrangement.

Finally, a move that brings either node to the ascendant can bring fame

So to sum up, moving to a location where the north node is rising would offer opportunities for karmic growth while one with the south node present would put you back into a previous (or perhaps a previous life) situation. Living with the north node rising would offer opportunities for advancement within the social and political lifestyle in the new location, while the south node rising would make it difficult for you to achieve your personal ambitions *unless you were careful to take local factors into consideration*. Thirdly, having either node rising would bring benefits in connection with property and family life. Lastly, I have noticed that anything that occurs on a chart and that involves the nodes brings a kind of fated or destined feeling about it. Therefore, if you were to move to such a spot, fate, destiny, kismet, karma and the wheel of fortune would all have a share in your new lifestyle.

The Set line

The set line is all about relating to other people, and as such, it offers information about the kind of relationships you can expect in your new location. You may act quite differently towards others in a fresh location and you may attract different types of people to you. New romances might emerge while stale relationships die off or perhaps a current one could simply change its character. This would partly be due to changes in your attitude or in the circumstances in which you and your lover find yourselves. Business and working relationships may be quite different from those in any other place and friendships may come, go or change.

The Sun set line

Remember that the set line is all about relationships with others and this works two ways, in that it reflects how you treat others and how they act towards you.

When you have read through this section, go back and read the section on the sun's rise line as this will add a great deal to your knowledge of the action of the sun on any line.

In this location, you might find yourself thrust into the center of social life and you would be able to impress, amuse or astound others with your increased charisma, but you may also be viewed as being too full of yourself or apt to put on airs and graces. You could also attract this kind of charismatic, self-centered folk to you and these people might expect you to become part of their own private appreciation society. One thing is certain, you won't be alone for long with the sun setting, and if there has been a famine in your love life or working life, this will surely be over. Marriage-type partnerships should be successful here and notwithstanding the usual ups and downs of life, you should be happy here.

You should draw 'sunny' cheerful, outgoing and generous people to you at this location and your own attitude would become more cheerful. Your friends would be the kind who see life as a game and they could encourage you to become the king or queen of whatever circle you start to move in. You may become the leader of the line dance class, a sporting star or a romantic river-boat gambler. Friendships, working relationships and the general atmosphere around you would encourage you to develop your creativity, so if there is something you have long wanted to do, you can get on with it here. You may be stimulated into starting a family, building a business of your own or promoting the talents of the creative people whom you meet here.

A mentor or a father figure could become part of your life at this location. You yourself could take on this role, especially if you decide to work with or to spend time with children or young people. You may decide to start a family of your own or you could become involved with someone else's family. Love affairs are a strong possibility and as long as you enjoy the thought of a hectic love life, this would be fine. If you are the type who wants a deeply committed relationship, this should work out very well too.

You would be encouraged to become more competitive at this location and whatever happens, it won't be other people who hold you back or prevent you from becoming a success. So taken all round, this should be a good place to live and an even better one in which to take a holiday.

The Moon set line

Remember that the set line is all about relationships with others and this works two ways, in that it reflects how you treat others and how they act towards you.

When you have read through this section, go back and read the section on the moon's rise line as this will add a great deal to your knowledge of the action of the moon on any line.

Helping others is the name of the game here but you would also need more than the usual amount of help and sympathy for yourself, as it would be difficult to maintain an independent attitude here. If you are used to being alone, a sudden desire to become part of a family could lead you to seek marriage-type relationships. Whether you begin a new partnership or whether you take a current partner with you to your new location, there are two possible problem areas that you would have to watch out for. The first is that your partner and/or others who are around you could suddenly turn into a pond full of lame ducks. Another problem is that you could attract people who think they have a right to push you around. When the moon becomes prominent on an angle, you become more sensitive than usual, and therefore you should avoid bullying or insensitive types of people.

Mothers or mother figures may become an important factor here and a woman who moves to such a location might develop a sudden maternal instinct which leads her to start a family of her own. If you do become 'broody', try to ensure that you would be happy here over the long term, the same goes for any responsibility that you take over on behalf of other people's children.

Your working life would bring you close to a number of new people and you might fancy working in one of the caring professions, or acting as an unpaid counsellor. You would take an interest in domestic matters and others would help you to become a good cook or homemaker. You could develop a taste for business by linking up with someone who has a good idea or two and who could do with a partner. Finally, the past would begin to mean a great deal to you at this location and you could find yourself amongst historians, collectors or genealogists.

To sum up, your emotions would be hard to control but your increased sensitivity would make you a sympathetic listener. You must take care about whom you attract in order to see that there is give and take in any new partnership.

The Mercury set line

Remember that the set line is all about relationships with others and this works two ways, in that it reflects how you treat others and how they act towards you.

When you have read through this section, go back and read the section on Mercury's rise line as this will add a great deal to your knowledge of the action of Mercury on any line.

Your greatest need here would be to attract intellectual and interesting people into your circle and the chances are that you would achieve this ambition quite easily. Others would encourage you to join in the conversation and to hone your communications skills, because any work that you take up would involve liaising with others. You could find yourself among people who communicate for a living, such as telephonists, journalists, drivers, receptionists and so on. Business relationships should prosper here and friendships would proliferate. If you have never learned to drive, use a computer or deal with tools and machinery, you would be encouraged to do so now. Mercury is often associated with health and healing, so you may find yourself among people who are interested in a healthy lifestyle. The worst case scenario could be that you find yourself caring for someone who is sick.

You may find yourself close to brothers, sisters or friends who become like siblings to you. Personal relationships would become less intense and your need for sex or passion may drop away to some extent as your need for mental attachments grows. Those whom you attract would probably prove to be more successful as friends or friendly, understanding and talkative lovers who don't really want a commitment. You may not want much of a commitment yourself at this location. Flirting and a measure of personal freedom may be more appealing than a settled relationship. Sitting down with a cuppa and a good book would also appeal to you here!

The Venus set line

Remember that the set line is all about relationships with others and this works two ways, in that it reflects how you treat others and how they act towards you.

When you have read through this section, go back and read the section on Venus's rise line as this will add a great deal to your knowledge of the action of Venus on any line.

If you wish to find a marriage-type partner, this is a good place to look for one! Venus is all about relating and when it is setting at your chosen location, you can forget all about being alone. If you like space and want nothing more than your own company, this is not the place for you. If you are seeking a well-heeled partner you could find him or her here.

Your charm and charisma increase here, and your social life would improve beyond measure. The folk you attract to you would be beautiful, fashionable, artistic, musical or just plain good company. You would feel an urge to be in attractive surroundings and to avoid those whose tastes and habits are vulgar. Life should be pleasant, relaxed and enjoyable and the lovely atmosphere would smooth the lines out of your face and actually make you look and feel better. You could become rather idle yourself at times, but the desire for a good lifestyle and your anxiety to have lovely things around you would keep your mind to some kind of money-making grindstone. The place itself should be attractive and peaceful or maybe it is just the people at this location who make it feel that way.

If you work at this location, your work would bring you into contact with women. It may take you into the beauty trade or into the kind of atmosphere you find in art galleries, musical events or classy and up-market places. The gym, the beauty salon, nice shops and your local squash and racquet club may become your second home. You and your lover would spend time in nice hotels and good restaurants.

Oddly enough, Venus setting can bring disputes into your life. This may either be due to the behavior of others or possibly because you take up arms against an injustice or two. You may attract people who argue but at least this would be stimulating. If your new location also brings a more pushy planet such as Mars into play, this would be a good place to live, but otherwise, this would make a lovely holiday destination or a good rest-cure spot. Go on, treat yourself to a seaweed wrap, a dose of reflexology and a facial, you would feel sooooo much more relaxed!

The Mars set line

Remember that the set line is all about relationships with others and this works two ways, in that it reflects how you treat others and how they act towards you.

When you have read through this section, go back and read the section on Mars's rise line as this will add a great deal to your knowledge of the action of Mars on any line.

Mars on any line brings energy, activity and a grand opportunity for fools to rush in where angels fear to tread! If you are unattached, you could very soon find yourself a partner but whether the relationship would be worth having depends upon your point of view. Such a relationship would not be boring and it could actually be a lot of fun. Sex would be a large issue here and as such, it could be a focus of great joy to you and your lover or it could cause you much trouble. Passions would run high and apart from sex, passionate feelings could be diverted into some joint venture that you get drawn into.

This line could also bring you furious arguments with both loved ones and outsiders.

If you want a relationship that makes you feel alive, then move to this location post haste! However, if you want a quiet life, maybe it would be better to stay away. Others would encourage you to succeed and they could validate you nicely by telling you how good you really are. You may also find yourself surrounded by men at this location or you could work in a place that uses lots of male labor. A friend of mine moved to her Mars set line and made a goodly number of gay male friends. Friendships are fun here and they should allow space and freedom on both sides.

You may take up a job in engineering, surgery, metalwork, the motor trade or even butchery! Or you could meet those who work in these trades. Teaching is a possibility here as is any kind of large working organization such as work for the armed services, the police or the civil service. You may not work in these fields, but you may come into contact with those who do. Either way, energetic, sporty, outgoing folk would become part of your circle and they would encourage you to try things you have never done before.

The worst aspect of this line is that arguments and even violent fights are possible and you would have to choose your partners, lovers and friends with care. Accidents are possible and driving could be especially dangerous here, as would be sudden inflammatory ailments.

All in all, a very stimulating line to visit or to do business in, but your basic nature is the criterion as to whether or not you'd like to stay on this line permanently.

The Jupiter set line

Remember that the set line is all about relationships with others and this works two ways, in that it reflects how you treat others and how they act towards you.

When you have read through this section, go back and read the section on Jupiter's rise line as this will add a great deal to your knowledge of the action of Jupiter on any line.

Jupiter on any line is usually considered a very nice thing but it can cause disruption in unexpected ways. For instance, if your life has been stuck in a cul-de-sac, Jupiter would bring the kind of losses and setbacks that force you to re-evaluate things and then to make some pretty extensive changes. Partnerships and love relationships may come to an end, allowing new ones to flourish. If you start out on your own at this location, you should find no difficulty in attracting friends or new business associates. Marriages here should be happy, lucky and full of fun and laughter. There may be financial benefits to be gained from marriage (or divorce) at this location.

Some kind of religious conversion is possible here and if this is the case, it would be due to the kind of people you run up against. You yourself may become a teacher or a religious leader who is looked up to by others, but if you become attracted to someone who is a kind of guru, make sure that you keep your mind open and your feet on the ground. A wonderful breakthrough in your spiritual life is possible but there could also be great damage done to the logical and sensible sides of your personality here.

Work may come your way in the form of teaching or something of a spiritual nature. You may take the opportunity of learning (or teaching) another language. The travel trade might appeal. You could simply attract those who work in these professions. Jupiter usually brings foreigners into one's life but if you are moving to another country, this is definitely on the cards. Legal matters and legal disputes should be easily settled here and you could even find work in a legal field of some kind. There would be opportunities for business partnerships here and you could find yourself acting in an international or a legal capacity as a result. All in all, Jupiter makes for an interesting and lucky life with plenty of fun, laughter and new interests to keep you amused.

The Saturn set line

Remember that the set line is all about relationships with others and this works two ways, in that it reflects how you treat others and how they act towards you.

When you have read through this section, go back and read the section on Saturn's rise line as this will add a great deal to your knowledge of the action of Saturn on any line.

Saturn has such a terrible reputation when setting that I became depressed at the thought of having to write this section, but when I stopped and thought about the many natal charts that I have analyzed that have Saturn on the descendant, the story is quite different. One thing to bear in mind is that Saturn rules the concept of *time*, so you do learn to take your time over things here and not to rush into anything, especially love, marriage or business relationships.

You can have a perfectly good marriage, love relationship or business partnership with Saturn on this line and the good news is that such a relationship would last. The message here is that all relationships must be taken seriously, because if you get into one that is difficult, it will take a long time before you can climb back out of it. You must guard against picking the kind of partner who is boring, heavy going, a workaholic or who puts you down and saps your confidence, but you must also guard against this kind of behavior in yourself. Business partnerships should be very good although you may end up with a nitpicker who is too cost conscious. Money can be made in such partnerships but it would be a long time before it does; losses should be small and easily containable.

Sure, you may pick a sick or a worrisome lover or someone who is less than a barrel of laughs, but who knows, this may be just what you want! A colleague of mine has Saturn setting in his natal chart and he still lives near where he was born, so this is continually operating. He has many good friends and plenty of short-term romances, but he doesn't want to live permanently with anyone.

Age differences are possible here and you may find yourself connecting in many different kinds of relationships and friendships with those who are older or younger than yourself. You could find a good mentor here or you may play that role with someone else, and finding or becoming a parental figure is also possible. Ambition would rise to the surface here.

The Uranus set line

Remember that the set line is all about relationships with others and this works two ways, in that it reflects how you treat others and how they act towards you.

After reading this section go back and read the piece about Uranus's rise line as this will give you much more additional information about the nature of Uranus and its effects on any angle.

You are likely to make some pretty drastic changes in your closest personal relationship when you move to this location and even a short holiday could have an effect. You would see your situation for what it really is and if it isn't any good, you won't be able to deny this fact. If your relationship or marriage is good and if you and your partner have enough space to be yourselves within the relationship, then this move should add a bit of zest and excitement to your current happiness. However, even within this situation, such a move might still bring to light a few uncomfortable realities and some unexpectedly unpleasant thoughts and feelings.

In the worst case, an established relationship might break up but new ones could also be quickly formed and if so, these would be very different from anything that you have experienced in the past. Your own attitude would become more independent and you would not want to be controlled or clung to by a partner. New people of all kinds would come rushing into your life and new attachments can be formed almost overnight but they could be very short lived, breaking up again just as quickly. Stability in any relationship would be hard to find and a certain amount of self-possession, independence and the ability to function on your own wouldn't come amiss here.

Uranus is especially concerned with acquaintanceships and group activities, so friendships and also a wider circle of friends are likely to be found here. Your new pals would be interesting and unusual and the normal conventions in life may not apply to them or to your relationships with them. This would be the world of the hippie commune, of free love and sexual experimentation, and indeed, also of celibacy. Mental rapports would be more important to you here than emotional ones. If a relationship does succeed on an emotional level, the sexual side may still be unconventional. Another possibility is that you have one partner who supplies one side of your emotional, mental and physical needs and another who fulfils other requirements. You may share yourself out at this place! New friends, lovers, business associates or colleagues would be intellectual, interesting, exciting, humorous and great fun. If your life is in a rut, such people would pull you out of it fast. Your own attitude would change to a more freedom-orientated and mental one, and your mind would be filled with stimulating ideas. Your own level of intelligence and education would increase and you could become qualified in a completely new field, doing something that you had never even considered before your move. The pace would be fast.

You would join or start groups and organizations and these could be of benefit to those who live in your new locality. Fund-raising, charity work, teaching and any other kind of committee or group activity are likely. You would want time to yourself to think and to study, so a number of friendships that also allow you the freedom to shut your door and to be alone at times would be the best. Working partnerships would be quite successful - if also rather volatile - and much depends upon a combination of your own basic nature and the kind of work that you choose to do. To clarify this a little, if you are a naturally steady, plodding, thorough and rather slow individual who decides to open a business or to work in a modern fast-moving trade, you could hitch up with exactly the right kind of exciting, eccentric, inventive, mentally energetic person here. Such a balanced partnership could be a great success, due to its mixture of charisma and common sense.

To sum up, this is a great place for a really exciting new love affair or for a major change of life but unless you are the reincarnation of Mau Tse Tung, permanent revolution would be very uncomfortable to live with over the long term. Move here to change your life and then perhaps find somewhere more relaxed and comfortable to live, unless perhaps you are a very Aquarian type of person who would enjoy the unsettled conditions that you find here.

The Neptune set line

Remember that the set line is all about relationships with others and this works two ways, in that it reflects how you treat others and how they act towards you.

After reading this section go back and read the piece about Neptune's rise line as this will give you much more additional information about the nature of Neptune and its effects on any angle.

Romance would come drifting into your life in this location and you may have the most memorable and wondrous love affair of all time. You and your new soul mate would find that your hearts beat in unison and that everything is beautiful, lovely and utterly unworldly. However, none of this would translate back into the real world of earning a living, changing nappies, fixing the car or doing the ironing! Even if you are the most practical type, this location could turn your heart and mind to jelly. This would be a lovely place to get away from it all, to have the holiday of a lifetime in and to have the love affair of all creation in, but it would be difficult to get anything done if you were to remain here for any length of time.

If you are very lucky, you could live or work with a very artistic or spiritual person but you would have to be prepared to earn enough to keep the pair of you in comfort and also to nurture and comfort your fragile lover through his or her mental and emotional ups and downs. Despite the unrealistic feeling about all this, it could still work out well - despite all logic. The downside is that you may see a potential lover through rose-colored glasses, seeing what you want them to be rather than the waste-of-space that they turn out to be. You must keep a very clear head and a sense of proportion here. You may be persuaded to cough up money for mad schemes or to become involved in chaotic and convoluted situations that you would later regret. The problem is that when your heart starts talking, your brain may switch off completely. Business relationships could be equally chaotic and you must avoid being openly or inadvertently swindled at this location. Don't go into anything that you cannot cope with here.

The good side of this location is that it brings you into contact with very talented people and this encourages you to take up art, gardening, music and creative work of all kinds. Spiritual people would surround you and your mind and your awareness would be opened to an extent that you might only previously have dreamed of. You would have psychic experiences at this location and you might develop mediumistic tendencies yourself. Any such gifts, especially healing ability would be brought out. You could join a religious, spiritual or philosophical sect or even a witch's coven! Some less ethereal but equally Neptunian possibilities would come your way through the people with whom you connect. For example, you could take up sailing or fishing or you could become interested in the production or sale of videos. Photography, films and music would become part of your life and you would come into contact with talented people who do such things. You could become involved with a poetry or theatre group or you could become a cinema projectionist. Finally, you would get a great deal of joy out of keeping small animals.

To sum up, if you want to be among talented, artistic or spiritual people who love the sea, this is the place for you. However, life would not be straightforward, and despite your own growing awareness and the number of wise folk with whom you come into contact, personal relationships are unlikely to be reliable. Neptune setting would be easier to live with if there were other more practical planets around but who knows, you may be a Piscean type of person who is suited to an unstructured way of life.

The Pluto set line

Remember that the set line is all about relationships with others and this works two ways, in that it reflects how you treat others and how they act towards you.

After reading this section go back and read the piece about Pluto's rise line as this will give you much more additional information about the nature of Pluto and its effects on any angle.

Pluto on any line takes a lot of living with and you would need to avoid becoming involved with manipulative and coercive types of people at this location. Your own feelings would intensify here and you would also draw intense people to you. Love relationships would be highly charged affairs with plenty of deep feelings involved. However, some of these deep feelings may be hard to live with, whether these emotions belong to you or whether you inspire them in others. Here we are looking at a strong potential for jealousy, obsession, rage and fury, fierce arguments (possibly accompanied by violence) and lots and lots of sex - or conversely, no sex at all! If you really want to live on the edge and to experience all that life has to offer, spend a little time at this location; but if you want to reach a peaceful old age, move away after a short time.

You can make some very good business contacts here, especially if you connect with people of influence and wealth. Money can be made in joint ventures at such a location and this would actually be a very good place for business of all kinds. It would probably be best to set up a business here and live elsewhere. Trades that might appeal to you here could be innovative recycling methods that transform things into other things. One example might be of making flower pots out of old garbage cans, or of making a derelict site into a health farm or a holistic and psychic centre.

The atmosphere around you could be politically unstable and dangerous, and you may even find yourself living in transformative and extremely difficult times. If you are an investigative journalist or a war reporter, this is exactly the right place for you. Even if your own life is peaceful you would draw crooks, political types and those who want to change the world into your immediate circle.

So to sum up, a Pluto line could suit heavily Scorpionic types or those who want good sex and a rich business life - but living here would require very steady nerves.

The Chiron set line

Remember that the set line is all about relationships with others and this works two ways, in that it reflects how you treat others and how they act towards you.

After reading this section go back and read the piece about Chiron's rise line as this will give you much more additional information about the nature of Chiron and its effects on any angle.

Moving to a location where Chiron is setting is likely to be very educational but the knowledge and experiences that come out of this would be very hard won. At best you would attract those to you who teach you new things. You may find a business mentor, a spiritual guru or someone who can show you how to grow prize leeks! You yourself may take up teaching as a career or you could find yourself acting as a mentor or guide to others. Love relationships may be confusing as they bring as much trouble with them as they do benefits but you would certainly learn something from these. Friendships may be based on teaching and learning or on shared interests and there is no doubt that any new friends would be bright and educated. You could learn a lot simply by being in a very different country or a very different culture from your own.

You may have to deal with sick people here and you could fall ill yourself. If you are ill before you arrive here, you would find just the right physician, therapist or practitioner to help you get better. An interest in health or healing could develop as a result of your experiences at this location. Through Chiron's association with the martial arts and also with music, I guess that you could become a guitar-playing karate expert at this location!

To sum up, personal relationships won't be easy but one way or another, you would learn new skills as a result of living with difficult people. You would learn and possibly teach others and you could become involved in health and healing as a career. If you have an urge to study or to engage in research, this place would help you to concentrate and also to open your mind to new ideas.

The set lines of the Moon's Nodes

Remember that the set line is all about relationships with others and this works two ways, in that it reflects how you treat others and how they act towards you.

After reading this section go back and read the piece about the rise line of the nodes as this will give you much more additional information about the nature of the nodes and their effects on any angle.

As explained earlier, the nodes do have a karmic or fated element to them, so if part of your soul's journey is to learn about relationship issues, you would do so at this location. This is not to say that your relationships with others would be especially difficult, it is just that they would help you to develop as a person. I guess that if you move to a location where the south node is setting, you would find yourself back in a situation that feels familiar - for good or ill. If you move to one where the north node is setting, your circumstances should be new and different.

Friendships would also have a fated feeling about them and these would work out pretty well. Business partnerships or arrangements would either be in a new and exciting field that is difficult to break into (north node) or an old established one that is easy to cope with (south node). Love relationships could be a bit difficult at times, but probably no more than is usual. Property matters that involve other people would be very successful for you here.

The MC line

The Sun MC line

For the characteristics of any sun line, go back and read the section on the sun's rise line as this will add greatly to the information that is given here. When looking at the MC line of any planet, bear in mind that this rules one's aims, ambitions and goals in life. In astrology, this is usually taken to mean career goals, but not everyone wants a career so this could mean any kind of ambition or search for status.

Career: The sun is specifically associated with visible success and achievement, so a career that allows you to reach the top would interest you and you would find it easier to climb the ladder of success here than anywhere else. Your success would be visible and it might bring you before the public in some way, for example in some form of show-business. Depending upon your basic nature as shown in your natal chart, you may be interested in climbing the corporate ladder or in becoming a top civil servant. Politics could interest you but only if there were strong political indicators on your chart; the Sun in Aries for example. You may suddenly decide to go it alone and start a business of your own, especially in a glamorous or exciting profession. You may become interested in working in the fields of fashion, jewelry, interior decorating, large construction enterprises or anything to do with computers. You may fancy starting and operating an airline - on the other hand, you may want to breed top dogs. It all depends on your basic nature but either way, self-promotion, a strong image and the gambler's instinct would become stronger features of your nature.

Non-career: Hobbies that might take your fancy could be dancing, art and craft work and anything to do with children and young people. You may wish to give up work for a while in favor of bringing up a family instead. If you have any creative urges these would come to the fore allowing you to make or create anything that comes out of your own imagination. You may become the leading light in a particular circle and you could become the host with the most, being noted for your wonderful home and delightful hospitality. Whatever you do would have a touch glamour and it would be fun.

The good news is that you have more chance of success in any endeavour at this location, but the bad news is that by concentrating on your goals so much, you could alienate your friends and your family. You must learn to keep a sense of proportion and a sense of balance between all sides of your life. You may become snobbish, arrogant or obstinate, particularly in your attitude to a career. Another possible problem is that you could have trouble with your parents or your children at this location. The MC and IC can relate to parents or parental figures in astrology, while the sun relates to children, so these issues could be brought to the forefront for good or ill as a result of a move to this line.

The Moon MC line

For the characteristics of any moon line, go back and read the moon's rise line section as this will flesh out the information that is given in this section. When looking at the MC line of any planet, bear in mind that this rules your aims, ambitions and goals in life. In astrology this is usually taken to mean career goals, but not everyone wants a career so this could mean any kind of ambition or search for status and success.

Career: Traditional astrology would indicate that the moon is far more concerned with home and family life than work, but if a career is chosen, then it could be in one of the caring professions or in something that benefits the public as a whole. This is true as far as it goes, but any planetary MC line adds ambition to even the most modest of career aspirations. A Moon line could incline you to making a career out of domestic skills, thus taking you into catering, soft furnishing or something similar. Producing or selling those things that interest women would work well here, so hairdressing, working in a gift shop or even reading Tarot cards might appeal. Counselling or medical work or indeed, anything that helps the sick or unhappy may attract you. An interest in history, antiques or anything that is attached to the past could be turned into a career, as could selling things that people collect. Small businesses and shop work would be successful too, as would any job that involves dealing with the public or appearing before the public via the media.

Non-career: Obviously all of the above mentioned items can be done as a form of unpaid social work or domestic work but at this location, you may decide to give up work to look after children or to care for an elderly parent. You may take yourself on some kind of inward journey and the enlightenment that you gain could be turned around to help others at a later date.

The only real danger of living on this line is that you might become too emotionally involved with your work or your interests, possibly neglecting your private needs as a result. You may also be so keen to help others that you sacrifice too much of yourself and your own needs in the meantime. There may be some problem relating to parents due to the fact that the MC and IC lines relate to parents while the moon itself is specifically concerned with mother figures.

One last word of caution is that the emotions and the career can become wrapped up in each other, therefore such dangerous and painful situations as falling in love with a superior, a subordinate or a colleague at this location are possible, with all the consequences this kind of scenario can bring - especially if either or both of you are married to other people at the time.

The Mercury MC line

For the characteristics of any Mercury line, go back and read Mercury's rise line section as this will flesh out the information given in this section. When looking at the MC line of any planet, bear in mind that this rules your aims, ambitions and goals in life. In astrology, this is usually taken to mean career goals, but not everyone wants a career so this could mean any kind of ambition or search for status and personal success.

Career: Creating order out of chaos might appeal to you here! You would become more methodical and orderly but you may also try to take on more responsibility than you can handle. Any career that gives you scope for communicating with others would appeal to you at this location and this could encompass writing, selling, broadcasting or teaching. Mail order goods or newsletters through the mail or some kind of computer communications work could become an important issue. Another possible career idea is that of working in the field of health and healing; indeed, you may manage to integrate both healing and also communicating into one job at this location. Intellectual and mental activity would become important to you at this place and you would choose to do something that stretched your mind. Once you have grasped whatever new concept you look into, you may then turn this to good advantage by teaching it to others. Craft work or some kind of mechanical work that necessitates the use of tools might interest you at this place. Another possibility is that of research and analysis, possibly leading you to produce a book or a paper for a specialist group or organization. You may work very successfully with brothers, sisters or relatives of that kind.

Non-career: Obviously all the above ideas could be translated into some kind of hobby or spare time interest.

Therefore, newsletters, computers and raising money through sales or mail order for a charity might appeal. Friendships and dealings with neighbors would increase. You could have a lot of fun getting together with others to talk through the night and to think up activities that you could do in small groups. You may discover that you need new communications skills at this location, leading you to acquire them. For example, you may need to learn to drive under different rules or different conditions or you may want to get to grips with computers, email or the like. In all these cases, you would find it easy to acquire these skills at this location. Do-it-yourself work, car maintenance or anything else that requires the use of tools may become important to you here. You would get to know your neighbors and they would invite you to become involved in local activities. Odd as it might sound, you could even discover or acquire sisters and brothers or you could make new brother/sister relationships for yourself with a partner's siblings.

You may become so wrapped up with your work or your interests that you neglect your family and friends here. Due to Mercury's logical and unemotional nature, you may lose some of your own emotional sensitivity but whether this is a good or a bad thing depends upon your personal chart and your personal circumstances.

The Venus MC line

For the characteristics of any Venus line, go back and read the Venus's rise line section as this will flesh out the information that is given in this section. When looking at the MC line of any planet, bear in mind that this rules your aims, ambitions and goals in life. In astrology, this is usually taken to mean career goals, but not everyone wants a career so this could mean any kind of ambition or search for status and personal success.

Career: Venus is associated with love and personal relationships so it doesn't look on the face of it as though this would have much impact on your career goals, but when we look more closely, we will see that this isn't quite so. Venus is also associated with *values* or anything that you value. This could cover such concrete items as possessions, status symbols and money but it can also refer to abstract notions, such as time to spend as one wishes, freedom and independence, security and so on. If you want a really worthwhile job, this line is a good place to be. Better still, any job at this location would be in a nice situation with pleasant people and probably in a quality line of work.

Venusian work could take you into the building and gardening trade, the fashion industry, cosmetics, hairstyling and so on. Interior decorating, antique restoration and any form of art, music or anything attached to beautiful things would be fortunate for you here. However, Venus is also associated with anything of an intrinsic value and among other things, money comes into the picture. Thus, work in a stock exchange, a bank or any other place that deals with money would be good. Dealing with valuable or beautiful objects would also apply, although antiques per se are mainly associated with the Moon. The oddest things can be connected to this planet, for example, mirrors, venetian blinds and even venereal disease, but how these might fit into a career pattern is anybody's guess! You can turn musical talent, dancing skills or a good singing voice into a career here.

Non-career: Obviously many of the matters that have been mentioned in the previous paragraph could be turned into personal interests, with such things as making a nice home, creating a garden and getting involved in the arts and crafts being strong contenders. Singing, dancing and music would make good hobbies at this location.

There are a very few potential problems that could arise here, but I guess that you could become snobbish and status-conscious here, alternatively you might make money your god for a while. Laziness is always a possibility with Venus on the MC so if things come easily to you at first here, you may simply sit back and do nothing. One odd but positive possibility is that you could fall in love with someone whom you meet through work. If so, they would be well-heeled, attractive and pleasant. They may not be quite so pleasant when you get to know them well, because Venus can have a very argumentative and unpleasant side to it.

The Mars MC line

For the characteristics of any Mars line, go back and read Mars's rise line section as this will flesh out the information that is given in this section. When looking at the MC line of any planet, bear in mind that this rules your aims, ambitions and goals in life. In astrology, this is usually taken to mean career goals, but not everyone wants a career so this could mean any kind of ambition or search for status and personal success.

Career: Mars on any line adds assertion, performance and maybe even aggression, so it is easy to see that this would have a galvanizing effect on any career aims. You would strongly identify yourself with your work, doing your damnedest to make a success of yourself. Despite all this push and pioneering attitude you would do best in a large organization rather than in a small one or in self-employment. There are some circumstances in which small would be beautiful though, such as by running a small engineering company, anything to do with vehicles or maybe a small building or craft company of your own. You could become attracted to the military life or the police at this spot, or to a large educational establishment. In any of these cases, you would strive for promotion and you would probably get it.

There would be more connection with men than with women in this environment and if you yourself are female, you would become more assertive and 'masculine' here, at least in terms of your attitude to a career. Whichever sex you are, your ambitions would soar and you could even be drawn into the higher echelons of politics at this spot.

Non-career: Hobbies could take you into much the same realms as those that I have suggested in the career section. For example, you might become involved with military cadets or such organizations as the scout movement. You may take up metalwork or car maintenance as a hobby or do-it-yourself work might suddenly appeal to you. Teaching and politics are also strong possibilities.

Problems might arise from an increasingly pushy or aggressive attitude. If male, you would become a real 'man's man' and maybe even something of a chauvinist pig! Oddly enough, both sexes would be tempted spend a lot of money on their appearance here! If you value your family life, you would enjoy this even more at this spot and, as long as you don't become too caught up in your job or your interests, your sex life would improve.

The Jupiter MC line

For the characteristics of any Jupiter line, go back and read Jupiter's rise line section as this will flesh out the information that is given in this section. When looking at the MC line of any planet, bear in mind that this rules your aims, ambitions and goals in life. In astrology, this is usually taken to mean career goals, but not everyone wants a career so this could mean any kind of ambition or search for status and personal success.

Career: Jupiter is supposed to bring success to any aspect of one's life that it touches but in my experience there are also times when it can destroy an existing situation, thus allowing or encouraging a new one to emerge. Sometimes the new career arises out of desperation, but despite my rather gloomy interpretation of the facts, what eventually *does* emerge, is invariably better and more meaningful than what went before. You may not actually want to make a success in the usual sense of increased status and more money at this location, because your inner motives could become directed towards spiritual aims and inner satisfaction instead.

You may find yourself becoming attracted to *Jupiterian* careers which could lead you into studying law or such subjects as religion and philosophy. These subjects require a great deal of study, a good memory and the ability to push back mental boundaries and to explore ideas by reasoned argument. Living close to such a line might bring you close to animals and you may decide to work with them at this location. Jupiter is also connected to travel, foreigners and foreign goods, so dealing with all these could become a part of your working life, especially if you have actually relocated yourself to a foreign country. Publishing and broadcasting are also possible at this location.

As I said in the previous paragraph, Jupiter is supposed to bring luck so even if you do start out with a setback or two, luck should soon come your way. Any enterprise that is started here would grow quickly, maybe *too* quickly unless something else kicks in to hold back the rush. Your own attitude would be more cheerful and optimistic than before and this would have a beneficial effect on those with whom you have any dealings. You may be far less attracted to material advantages there than the feeling that you are doing the right thing. If spiritual advancement is your thing, you could soon find yourself administering healing to the public, giving clairvoyance from a platform at the local Spiritualist Church or becoming an astrologer. If you enjoy teaching you could do well at it in this place and if you want to work in show-business, this too should be successful.

Non-career: Many of the above-mentioned ideas could be turned into spare time activities. Studying and even teaching or training may be part of a hobby and spiritual development, however seriously it is taken, is not normally viewed as a road to financial success. Legal matters are less likely to become hobby material but studying them could be. You may take an interest in gambling and you could be very lucky here, especially if you gamble on horses. If you fancy trying your hand at amateur dramatics or any other kind of entertainment, you would have a lot of fun.

There are no real problems here but schemes and enterprises may move a bit too fast, bringing over-optimism and overexpansion. You might become arrogant and adopt a snobbish outlook, especially if you start to make money. If you meet a lover through your job at this place, he or she would be a success in their own right and they may even be rich! Better still, they would have a lovely sense of humor.

The Saturn MC line

For the characteristics of any Saturn line, go back and read Saturn's rise line section as this will flesh out the information that is given in this section. When looking at the MC line of any planet, bear in mind that this rules your aims, ambitions and goals in life. In astrology, this is usually taken to mean career goals, but not everyone wants a career so this could mean any kind of ambition or search for status and personal success.

Career: For all that Saturn has the reputation of being a miserable planet, it does have some saving graces and if you move to a place where Saturn's MC is located, you would find them. Saturn brings hard work and struggle, but it also brings success. If you make any kind of effort here, it would eventually be rewarded, but if you give up trying and simply sit back, you would simply sink into failure and depression. Saturn represents authority, reaching the top, the trappings of status and being taken seriously. In this location you would be able to call on a number of responsible senior people to help and advise you. Career possibilities could lead you into large organizations, banks or anything else that carries status and responsibility. Accountancy, bookkeeping and publishing are other possibilities but tree surgery, osteopathy and many other professions are equally possible here. Whatever you do here would require thoroughness, attention to detail and self-discipline. Oddly enough, writing would be a good career here, especially the kind of long book that requires a good deal of knowledge and research.

Non-career: It is hard to conceive of anyone living with Saturn on the MC *without* wanting to work but if circumstances made this impossible, I guess that one's ambition would be channelled in some other way. Perhaps other members of the family would be pushed and chivvied into succeeding, maybe snobbery and social status would become all consuming. Illness could be turned into a career with lots of emphasis being placed on finding the 'top' doctor or therapist. Maybe one would just live to become very old indeed here!

The problem of living on such a line is that a serious and practical attitude to work could be taken too far and the family and friends would be neglected as a result. A miserly attitude is also possible at this place. Another problem is that the sheer grind of any job could wear you down. Fame and glory could come but so could public disgrace, so straight dealings and a lack of skeletons in the cupboard is a must. If there is a choice, perhaps this would be a great place to work for a while on a contract basis but the main home should be kept somewhere else. If there are other softer planets also brought into play by moving to this location, this would be all well and good.

The Uranus MC line

For the characteristics of any Uranus line, go back and read Uranus's rise line section as this will flesh out the information that is given in this section. When looking at the MC line of any planet, bear in mind that this rules your aims, ambitions and goals in life. In astrology, this is usually taken to mean career goals, but not everyone wants a career so this could mean any kind of ambition or search for status and personal success.

Career: If you really want to throw up the career you already have and do something really different, this is the place for you! Uranus is such an unpredictable planet that it could lead you into almost any kind of job, especially an unusual one. Uranus is the break-out planet, so sudden changes of career or changes of direction are likely as a result of moving to this location. You may take two part time jobs or one career that has a great deal of variety attached to it. Studying or teaching might become part of your life, especially if you do decide on a real change of career. You may take up social work or you could become involved in a 'cause'. You would certainly be keen to help others and you could become deeply involved in the politics of any organization that you join. Counselling might appeal to you at this location. This sign is traditionally associated with electronics, radar, computers and airlines so work in any kind of high-tech profession would be a success. Astrology might appeal to you at this location and you could study to become a professional astrologer at this spot.

Non-career: Many of the above mentioned ideas can be turned into hobbies and interests but some involvement in local matters or any movement that seeks to preserve the environment or to improve conditions would appeal. Astrology would make a wonderful hobby here. Group activities, fund raising for clubs and societies would be great fun and you would certainly make many new friends. Voluntary or paid work for a local government organization would work out well here.

The only real problem of living on such a MC line is that you might become too unsettled and too apt to chop and change your job. You could also become too wrapped up with a cause and therefore lose your sense of proportion. Personal or sexual relationships may lose their appeal as you move towards a preference for friendships and less *attached* relationships.

The Neptune MC line

For the characteristics of any Neptune line, go back and read Neptune's rise line section as this will flesh out the information that is given in this section. When looking at the MC line of any planet, bear in mind that this rules your aims, ambitions and goals in life. In astrology, this is usually taken to mean career goals, but not everyone wants a career so this could mean any kind of ambition or search for status and personal success.

Career: A glib comment on moving to a Neptune MC line is that you *won't* have a career! However clever and amusing that comment might make me look, it simply isn't true. With Neptune on such a line, your values would be spiritual rather than material but you could be quite ambitious in your own way. You could be drawn to one of the caring professions such as nursing, looking after children or animals. Anesthetics are especially associated with this planet. Birds and fish would appeal to you in quite a big way here and you could make a living by breeding birds or catching fish. Creative jobs would appeal to you and anything to do with art, music and photography could be just the thing. It would be hard for you to focus steadily on your aims, and escapist thoughts or dreams may undermine your progress. You may look after handicapped folk and you might introduce them to dancing, swimming or the arts and crafts. Chiropody may appeal to you here and it is possible that the business of making or selling shoes or socks could apply!

Non-career: Obviously many of the ideas that I have suggested in the section before this one would apply but there is one more to consider and that is the idea of spiritual development. You could study the Tarot, psychic development, spiritual healing, astrology or any other spiritual or occult craft.

You would certainly be able to develop mediumistic or healing techniques at this location.

The danger of having Neptune on any line is that you may not be able to see the wood for the trees. You may become confused in your aims, unable to keep any kind of job going and unable even to keep your own energy level high enough to achieve anything. Neptune will send you on an inner journey which, depending upon your own natal chart, can either stay inside you or be turned to such career options as counselling or spiritual guidance. Romance may call you but this may come in the form of loving the romance of the seas, the jungle or the desert. You may become disillusioned by people or places in the end. If you fall in love through a work connection, such a liaison would very likely be filled with complications. You would have to keep a firm grip on such things as alcohol and drugs if these are not to be allowed to rule your life.

To sum up, any Neptune line would be great for a holiday, especially if this is on or by water. However, this is too vague a place in which to live and work, unless something far more practical in your basic character is also brought into play.

The Pluto MC line

For the characteristics of any Pluto line, go back and read Pluto's rise line section as this will flesh out the information that is given in this section. When looking at the MC line of any planet, bear in mind that this rules your aims, ambitions and goals in life. In astrology, this is usually taken to mean career goals, but not everyone wants a career so this could mean any kind of ambition or search for status and personal success.

Career: Typical Pluto careers are in the fields of investigation and in both the literal and the metaphoric sense of digging up anything that is hidden. Therefore on a practical level, work in mining, archaeology, the police, tracking down insurance fraudsters and psychic investigation would work well here. Power games and power struggles might apply, either as part and parcel of the kind of work that you find, or within any organisation that you choose to work in. Your own drive to influence others would grow at this location.

Big business and big money could become part of your life so jobs in banking, investment, the tax department or the stock exchange may be on offer. Legal work that deals with mortgages, taxation, legacies and divorce could also work well. This line could lead you into the deeper kinds of psychotherapy and mental investigations, with sex therapy as an obvious choice. As you can see, there is no shortage of jobs to be found on this line but the intensity of the work and the power struggles within it would take a lot of living with, unless you are that way inclined by nature.

Non-career: There is a professionalism to this line that makes it hard to turn many of the above mentioned career possibilities into hobbies. Even such matters as counselling would need to be on a deeper and professional basis. You can't really play at anything here, the line is far too serious. So if you do find yourself on such a line, you must either study and train for something deep and real or maybe take another route entirely and simply dig around and research some pet idea, possibly with the intention of writing a book about it at a later date.

Like the Neptune line above, there may be a danger of being drawn into the world of drink and drugs at this location, but criminality and even murder could enter your life in some way, directly or indirectly.

The Chiron MC line

For the characteristics of any Chiron line, go back and read Chiron's rise line section as this will flesh out the information that is given in this section. When looking at the MC line of any feature, bear in mind that this rules your aims, ambitions and goals in life. In astrology, this is usually taken to mean career goals, but not everyone wants a career so this could mean any kind of ambition or search for status and personal success.

Career: The myth of the Centaur god, Chiron, was that he was a teacher and also a physician of sorts. Chiron became wounded in one of his back legs by one of Hercules' misplaced arrows, and after swapping his mortality with Uranus, died and became a star in heaven. The point of this story is to show the careers that might be suggested by moving to a Chiron MC line. Teaching would have to be the thing and if you want to follow Chiron's example, the subjects would be athletics, martial arts, music and anything else that the ancient Greek world considered to be important. Healing, counselling, nursing and caring for others would also fit the bill here.

Non-career: Obviously all of the above mentioned ideas could be put to good use for helping out or teaching others, either for pin money or for no fee at all. Otherwise there really isn't much more to say about this.

Moving to any Chiron line would be likely to bring a certain amount of pain to the surface, so if you have suffered either in previous life or earlier on in this current life, you would bring this out into the open and sort it out once and for all. Once you have come to terms with whatever psychological problems have ailed you in the past, you could use this knowledge to add to your own store of wisdom and then perhaps go on and help others.

A potential problem could be, as with any Mc line, that you become so wrapped up in your work that you neglect your private life or that you work too hard.

The MC lines of the Moon's Nodes

For the characteristics of any node line, go back and read the rise line section for the nodes as this will flesh out the information that is given in this section. When looking at the MC line of any feature, bear in mind that this rules your aims, ambitions and goals in life. In astrology, this is usually taken to mean career goals, but not everyone wants a career so this could mean any kind of ambition or search for status and personal success.

It is not really possible to ascribe any particular career opportunity to the nodes of the moon but there are a few vague connections. The first is that the nodes may have a slightly similar effect to that of living on the moon's MC line, so it would be worth turning back the pages and scanning through that section. What is much more to the point is the Karmic or fated feel about any node line. Therefore, if you did move to any place where a node is on the line, you would be given an opportunity for inner growth and understanding of the soul's condition. There may be a destined feeling to life when you move to a node. Relationships that arise through work may be especially important to you and even the job you do, whatever it may be, could have a deeper meaning to it than just the means of earning some money.

Having said that, I have often noticed in ordinary predictive astrology that any planetary move to the nodes seems to refer to property matters. Buying, selling or renting property or premises could be a good job here. If this just happens as part and parcel of your move, it would be a success.

The north node would teach you the most as it leads to future growth, while the south node would take you back into a past (maybe even a past life) situation. This is a subtle and difficult matter to try to explain, but you would certainly feel the pull of destiny on either of these lines. Sometimes fame follows a move to one of the node lines, but if you prefer to be in control of your destiny, maybe think twice before moving permanently to such a location.

The IC line

The Sun IC line

The IC line refers to the home, domestic circumstances, family life, private life, also the influences of the past. A home should be comfortable and convenient and in the right location because the wrong home is unbearable to live in.

After reading through this section, you can discover more about the sun if you turn back and read through the section about the sun's rise line.

The sun endows success to any line, so this placement would make your home a happy and sunny place to be in and typically, children play a part in your life at this location. You may decide to settle down and raise a family of your own in this place, or you could become involved with other people's children one way or another. If you work from your actual home or from premises that are reasonably close to your home, this would work out satisfactorily for you. Your home would be comfortable and it could be slightly larger than the average for the area. This would be a great place to retire to, especially if there is a chance of having grandchildren or other family youngsters to stay. This is more likely to be an exciting and interesting location than a bucolic or sleepy one, so you really need to assess your own feelings before moving to this line, and to gauge whether you want to get away from it all or to be in the midst of everything.

The value of any property that you buy here would increase, and if you choose to rent a home or a workshop at this location, this would turn out to be good value for money. The chances are that you would settle down at this location and not move away again too quickly.

Although your emotional life depends upon many factors, there is as good a chance as any that living in such a spot would bring happiness. Issues of fatherhood may become important here for any number of possible reasons. For instance, you may decide to become a father at this location or you may develop a close relationship with someone who stands as a father figure. Females could marry a man who already has children and in this case, the relationship between the woman and her stepchildren would be very good and you could still go on to have children of your own within the family. Once you enter a relationship here, you'll try to make it last.

I can't really see anything negative about living in such a spot, except for the fact that you may place your home and family above a career - but so what? Secondly you may become ambitious and *pushy* towards your children or your partner, and this may rebound on you later when they get fed up with the pressure.

The Moon IC line

The IC line refers to the home, domestic circumstances, family life, private life, also the influences of the past. A home should be comfortable and convenient and in the right location because the wrong home is unbearable to live in.

After reading through this section, you can discover more about the moon if you turn back and read through the section about the moon's rise line.

The IC is the natural position for the moon on any chart so you ought to feel particularly *at home* in this location, finding just the kind of home you really want in a pleasing location. The chances are that the area would be peaceful and that there would be a body of water nearby, so if you are looking for shops and bright lights, this is not the place for you! If you want a non-stressful and attractive environment, this is definitely the right spot. Your emotions become stronger at this spot and you may begin to develop your intuition or your psychic perceptions here. If you are fairly cool in temperament to start with, this would be all to the good but if you are already overemotional or temperamental, it might not be wise to live here permanently.

Mothers, mother figures and motherhood issues would become important here. For example, you could find yourself looking after elderly female relatives or becoming close to a mother figure here. You may of course, decide to become a mother yourself here. If male, you may connect with a woman who is a mother or who is of a motherly disposition. Either sex could acquire stepchildren or even step-grandchildren and you would feel very comfortable with this. Nurturing, caring for others and even working from home in a teaching or caring capacity are all possible here. You would be able to find some peace here especially if you can sit by a pond, a river or the sea.

The past would exert some kind of influence at this location, so in simple terms, you may start to collect old objects or things that have a history to them. Your own memorabilia would become important to you and I guess you could even start to write your autobiography here!

The only real problem is related to the emotional and changeable nature of the Moon as this could throw your own emotional equilibrium out of balance or you might become so involved with looking after others that you neglect yourself.

The Mercury IC line

The IC line refers to the home, domestic circumstances, family life, private life, also the influences of the past. A home should be comfortable and convenient and in the right location because the wrong home is unbearable to live in.

After reading through this section, you can discover more about Mercury if you turn back and read through the section about Mercury's rise line.

If you want to live in splendid isolation with no neighbors and nobody disturbing your domestic tranquillity, then don't move to this location! Your home life would be busy here with plenty of friends and neighbors dropping in and your phone bills could be enormous. You would need to keep a good stock of paper, envelopes and stamps because communicating with others would be a very large part of your life here. You might work from home or if you don't work, you would become involved in local affairs, possibly through your children's school or through any kind of local club or group. Life would be busy but also very entertaining. You and your family would talk a lot with each other and most of the relationships in and around the home should be good. The property itself may not be large or particularly outstanding but it would be comfortable and suitable to your needs. You may not bother with a garden but there should be some nice countryside within easy reach.

If you run some kind of small business from your home or from premises that are close to your home, this would involve plenty of dealings with the public. You could work in some kind of liaison between people or in a counselling capacity. History and antiques would interest you here and you might take up something related to the past such as genealogy. Computers, fancy telephones and electronic communications equipment of all kinds would find their way into your home, and newsletters could pour out of it. Try to ensure that a post office and a letter box are close by because you would need them! You would also need a good transport system which should be a good mixture of public transport and a reliable vehicle of your own. Sales work, journalism or teaching from home would be successful here as would counselling or astrology.

There is no real drawback to living in this area except for the fact that you would feel restless at times. You must be free to come and go as you like or you would feel restricted and frustrated. Your family relationships may not be terribly romantic but there would be a good mental wavelength between all members of the family.

The Venus IC line

The IC line refers to the home, domestic circumstances, family life, private life, also the influences of the past. A home should be comfortable and convenient and in the right location because the wrong home is unbearable to live in.

After reading through this section, you can discover more about Venus if you turn back and read through the section about Venus's rise line.

If you want a really lovely home, this is the place to move to because the property should be peaceful, attractive, spacious and most likely valuable. You should have a lovely garden at this location and you should also live in an area surrounded by beautiful views and pretty countryside. Your home would be filled with lovely things. It is possible to make quite a bit of money at this location if you work from home or very close to where you live. Love would be all around you and life should be pleasant and easy. It would be easy to attract a lover here and any relationships you form here would be very romantic but also pretty secure. You would want to cook, garden or entertain in style and homemaking would become a pleasure here. Your outlook would be sensual and you would become far more sexy in this place too!

If you move your parents to this location or if you acquire in-laws, the relationships would be easy and the older generation could become rich here! If you become a mother figure yourself, you would be the lovely old-fashioned kind of earth mother. This would be a great place to raise children but also to become active in creative pursuits or in creating beauty in all its forms.

The only drawback here is that you could become lazy and fat! So if there are any such leanings within you, you should try singing, dancing or aerobics in this location; these are all good for the arteries and for keeping the body in shape.

The Mars IC line

The IC line refers to the home, domestic circumstances, family life, private life, also the influences of the past. A home should be comfortable and convenient and in the right location because the wrong home is unbearable to live in.

After reading through this section, you can discover more about Mars if you turn back and read through the section about Mars' rise line.

Mars is the most energetic of all the planets so I guess the first thing you would put into your home would be some exercise machinery! This is a softer placement for Mars than any of the others but it would still stimulate you into action. If you work from this location you would do very well, especially if the job required demonstrating things to others or some form of selling. Teaching and sports coaching would also be successful at this location. A business such as farming or engineering would be an excellent choice, especially if it were attached to the home or located close by.

Family life could go one of two ways. You might have a busy, lively family with plenty of men and boys around the place and lots of space for ball games and bikes. If so, you would have the time of your life with this family. However, if you are shoved into a maternal role in cramped surroundings, you won't cope. If you are placed in a purely domestic setting with no outlet for your brains and energy, you would go totally nuts here. You need space to get away from the family and to be yourself at times and you definitely need an outlet or some way of relieving your own inner tensions and passions here.

Relationships with older females would either be wonderful or terrible at this location.

Your sex life would improve, and if you aren't accustomed to taking the initiative in sexual matters, your partner would be in for a shock! However, your capacity for creating and keep up family arguments would increase mightily and you may start family fights as a way of staving off boredom. Whether other members of the family appreciate your newly discovered talent for mouth-karate would be a moot point! Any Mars line can attract violence so if you do move here, be sure to protect your property and your goods from theft and be sure to protect yourself from casual violence. If a relationship becomes truly acrimonious to the point of violence, either leave it or persuade your loved ones to move away.

I would recommend this spot for business dealings or for competitive sporting activities in preference to domestic life, but if you are an Aries or a Scorpio type, you would be able to cope with it, and perhaps love it!

The Jupiter IC line

The IC line refers to the home, domestic circumstances, family life, private life, also the influences of the past. A home should be comfortable and convenient and in the right location because the wrong home is unbearable to live in.

After reading through this section, you can discover more about Jupiter if you turn back and read through the section about Jupiter's rise line.

This would be a lively and interesting place to live in, both in terms of the area in general and your home in particular. There would be no shortage of exciting things to do. Your relationships with loved ones should be pretty good and if there is a mother or mother-figure nearby, you should get on very well with her. The property itself may cost more than you expected but it would be worth the expense and it should increase in value while you live there. Much the same goes for any business that you might choose to run in your home, but you would have to guard against becoming involved in get-rich-quick schemes. You may inherit property or gain it through a court case here. The chances are that a house would be spacious with a good deal of land surrounding it and it would be a great place in which to breed or keep animals of any description.

If you are moving away from your birth or natural country, you would enjoy being among foreigners and living a different kind of lifestyle from your previous one. Businesses that involve foreigners or foreign goods would prosper here. You may take up spiritual or healing arts here and if you give counselling or healing from your home this would be beneficial to those whom you treat and also to you yourself. This is a great place to take up a course of home study or from which to teach others.

About the only drawback that you might meet here is that you could have to take frequent trips away from your home on business or for some other reason, and this may be a little too tiring or dislocating for comfort. Conversely, if you are forced into staying put or if your situation is restricting in any way, you would become restless, leading you to look for ways of escaping or travelling. Another possibility is that you would have to adapt to a land where a different language is spoken or to religious and philosophical views that are very different from your own. Whether this becomes a source of fascination or a pain in the neck depends upon your own outlook on life and your own ability to adapt to a new environment.

Lastly, luck should surround you here and any enterprise you take up locally should go well, but you must guard against getting into anything too quickly without giving it enough thought, or expanding some enterprise further and faster than necessary.

The Saturn IC line

The IC line refers to the home, domestic circumstances, family life, private life, also the influences of the past. A home should be comfortable and convenient and in the right location because the wrong home is unbearable to live in.

After reading through this section, you can discover more about Saturn if you turn back and read through the section about Saturn's rise line.

Any Saturn line can be restrictive and troublesome so it may be as well to avoid trying to live permanently in this location, but if you are ambitious, this line would help you to achieve your aims in life, although nothing would come your way easily or quickly. Fathers and father figures would be a strong influence in this place and this could be a good thing, although this depends upon a variety of circumstances. You would develop a strong sense of responsibility here and you could find yourself taking on more than you had bargained for. However, achievements can be made and in time money can be made out of property dealings. You would certainly develop a practical and sensible attitude at this place but you could become somewhat dour, gloomy or tightfisted if you stayed here too long.

If you work from home, your job would require attention to detail and a good deal of self-motivation but it should be a success. Oddly enough, work with computers, writing, publishing and journalism would be good to take up at this location. Other careers here would involve dealing with money, and with valuable goods. Other possibilities could be osteopathy or beauty therapy, through Saturn's association with the bones and the skin.

Relationships formed here would last but they might not be a barrel of laughs. You may become depressed and it might be worth going into counselling or even having regression therapy to discover just what happened in your past (or your past life), to cause any onset of depression or unhappiness.

Poverty, hardship and difficult circumstances might well be
your lot if you choose to live here.

This would be a good place for serious business contacts
or for opening a distant branch of any business but it might
not be a good choice of place to live in for any length of time.

The Uranus IC line

*The IC line refers to the home, domestic circumstances,
family life, private life, also the influences of the past. A home
should be comfortable and convenient and in the right location
because the wrong home is unbearable to live in.*

*After reading through this section, you can discover more
about Uranus if you turn back and read through the section
about Uranus's rise line.*

The first thing to come to terms with if you move to this
line is that you may move away again much more quickly
than you had anticipated! Life would be unsettled here and
you may even find that you don't really get around to unpacking
before you have to travel again. If you do manage to settle
here, you can expect your home to be an unusual one, either
because it is a peculiar place to start with, or because you turn
it into an oddity yourself. You may fill your house with
computers, electronic equipment, a recording studio or
something of the kind. If you were to attach a school or a
centre of learning to your home, this would work very well.
You could learn or teach astrology at this location.

Friendships can be made and many acquaintanceships
would develop here. You would become involved in group
activities in or near your home and life would certainly be
interesting. Personal relationships might become unstable and
the chances are that you would fall out with mother figures or
that such mother types would be extremely eccentric. You may
put a strain on love relationships yourself due to an increasing
need for more than the usual amount of freedom and
independence, and if you have hitherto been a real homemaker

or possibly the family doormat, your nearest and dearest would all be in for a nasty shock!

The best that could be said about this line is that your children and other family members would soon learn to be independent at this location. You yourself would become less attached to close ties. You would also have more time to read, to think and to learn, and you could turn this input of knowledge to good advantage by teaching others or by becoming involved in local politics. To sum up, this would be an interesting place to visit for a while, especially if you intend to study, but it might be a bit too unsettling for permanent home life.

The Neptune IC line

The IC line refers to the home, domestic circumstances, family life, private life, also the influences of the past. A home should be comfortable and convenient and in the right location because the wrong home is unbearable to live in.

After reading through this section, you can discover more about Neptune if you turn back and read through the section about Neptune's rise line.

This is a great location in which to develop your creativity and to stretch your imagination, so writing, painting, gardening or any other such activity would enhance your life. If you create a garden here, the Neptune connection would encourage you to use water artistically as part of the scene. A home in this location could be a thing of beauty or a complete mess depending upon your mood at the time, and you may become so wrapped up in some project or other that you allow the place to go to rack and ruin. Alternatively, you could turn your home into an animal sanctuary that is alive with moggies and doggies! If this location is by the sea or by a body of water, this would give you plenty of opportunity for water-based activities such as boating, fishing, swimming or looking at the view and drawing or painting it.

This would be a great place for you to embark on a search for spiritual growth and to develop in an inward capacity. If you did reach outwards at all it would be by turning your home into some kind of centre or by inviting selected people to visit your private chapel or alter. You may lose yourself in the spiritual world to the extent that it becomes impossible for you to work or function in a normal manner. If you go completely overboard with your newfound karmic journey, you could easily alienate your friends and your loved ones, unless they are also interested in a spiritual lifestyle. You would become extremely sensitive here, both in the sense that your feelings would be easily aroused and also in the psychic and intuitive sense.

You would have to guard against taking on lame ducks or becoming used by stronger people for their own ends. In all things, a sense of proportion would be needed. To be honest, it would be a good thing if you had one or two other more practical planets involved in this location as well as Neptune itself. Escapist activities might encroach too much on your mind and your life to the point where alcohol, drugs and obsessive or peculiar traits would need to be curbed. You would also need to guard against becoming self-pitying or becoming a victim at this location.

This location could lead to a wonderful flowering of creativity and it would bring you peace if you have been through a troubled or restless phase, but it may be too chaotic or nebulous for practical day to day life. Spiritual development and the art of giving to others are wonderful, but living for others can become too much of a way of life here for your own mental health. Any love relationships that develop here would be of the most romantic and dreamy kind, but the absence of reality or of a realistic attitude could result in them ending in disillusionment and broken dreams. The trouble is that Neptune can act as a kind of acid that dissolves everything that it comes into contact with, so all those things that you thought were set in concrete, such as your family, your money or your household goods, can slip away though your fingers. Neptune can also feel as though fate were doing a kind of dance of the seven veils, thus making you aware of what is really going on in the hearts and minds of those around you. This is due to the developing intuition and psychic awareness that comes whenever Neptune is nearby.

The Pluto IC line

The IC line refers to the home, domestic circumstances, family life, private life, also the influences of the past. A home should be comfortable and convenient and in the right location because the wrong home is unbearable to live in.

After reading through this section, you can discover more about Pluto if you turn back and read through the section about Pluto's rise line.

This is not an ideal place for anyone to live in, but if you are a Scorpio or if you have Pluto strongly marked on your own horoscope, you would cope with it better than most. The problem is that issues such as control, bullying, dictating to others, or being on the receiving end of such behavior, would raise themselves here. Your own feelings would intensify and some of these could become extremely uncomfortable. Power struggles could go on in or around the home. A typical scenario would be the kind that comes before, during and after a divorce. Power struggles between generations could occur. You may or may not be able to take charge of your own home due to some other relative being foisted upon you.

Worse than this, you might lose your home, your family and your money as a result of debts, losses, disagreements, divorce, local violence, illness or death. On the other hand, Pluto can bring great gains in the form of money, legacies, divorce procedures, marriage, union in business and with groups and in many other ways. Nothing would be lighthearted or easy going here and whether it is love, hate, jealousy, fear, distress, ecstasy or anything else that you feel here, you would feel it to the utmost.

If you want to change the shape of your domestic and family life, then move to this area and allow Pluto to destroy, rebuild and recycle your life for you. If you want things to stay just as they are, then keep away. If you want to go deeply into yourself in any way, this is the place to do it. Psychological analysis, hypnotic regression and any other deep form of psychic and psychological delving would help in this location. However, once you have achieved the aim of finding the roots of your problems and then setting about putting them right, it would be just as well to move to a less traumatic area. The same goes for psychic matters. You would open up psychically in such a place and this could be an excellent thing to do, but it would take a strong, resilient personality to live permanently on a Pluto line.

The Chiron IC line

The IC line refers to the home, domestic circumstances, family life, private life, also the influences of the past. A home should be comfortable and convenient and in the right location because the wrong home is unbearable to live in.

After reading through this section, you can discover more about Chiron if you turn back and read through the section about Chiron's rise line.

Chiron is associated with teaching and healing, so if you dream of running a holistic centre or a school from your home or from a place that is close by, this would be an excellent choice. If you enjoy studying or teaching, you would be successful here. Chiron can be associated with deep psychological wounds so I guess that if you want to dig down deep and put right those things that have been bugging you for years, this would be the place to go. The same goes for rooting out a long-standing ailment. You would find teachers, healers, guides and helpers here, but it may be as well to move away again once you have got to the heart of the matter and started your healing journey, as you don't want to keep on dredging up past hurts or past mistakes. If you do stay in this location, then you must use the knowledge you have gained by delving into your own psyche in order to help others, that way you would be making a positive use of this line at this location.

As this location really affects your home and family life, it might be worth bearing in mind that Chiron can bring ill health to you and to those whom you love. Such ailments would become part and parcel of a period of self-discovery, self-awareness and lessons of one kind or another but, to be honest, who needs to be ill to find out what life is all about?

The IC lines of the Moon's Nodes

The IC line refers to the home, domestic circumstances, family life, private life, also the influences of the past. A home should be comfortable and convenient and in the right location because the wrong home is unbearable to live in.

After reading through this section, you can discover more about the nodes if you turn back and read through the section about nodes' rise line.

There are three theories associated with the nodes of the moon that I have covered in the rise line section, but I will briefly mention them again here. The first is that they have a karmic or fated feel to them owing to the fact that the north node is supposed to represent the karmic future while the south node is supposed to represent the karmic past. The second idea is of social or political atmospheres, where your north node is in tune with these and the south node is out of tune. The third is strictly to do with the home, the family and the domestic situation, so let us take all three of these, mainly concentrating perhaps on the last item.

So firstly, karma. As this area represents your private inner world and the domestic side of things, you may feel that fate is commanding this area of your life and that you lose the ability to take control if it. If you move to the north node's IC line, your fate would move you forward to face new challenges, while if you move to the south node's IC line, you might be faced with a repeat of a previous situation.

Secondly, politics and the social arena. If you move to a location on your north node's IC line, the way you want to live and to run your home would fit in with local ideas. For example, your neighbors' way of life, the schools your children go to, the way you are expected to dress, to run your home or to behave generally would be much the same as those who are around you. If you move to a south node IC line, this could be very uncomfortable and strange. Imagine moving to Japan, Cambodia, Greenland or somewhere else equally bizarre and you will soon see what I mean.

Thirdly, as far as I can see, either node would be good for domestic and property matters but it might be better to move to a north node line than a south node one. Either way, you could expect to find just the right place at just the right price and to have a happy and comfortable home life. The family finances improve and you would feel in your private life at least, that you are going with the flow.

Local Space Map Astrology

What are Local Space Maps and how do they work?

Local Space Maps are a system of geographic astrology that has its roots in celestial navigation. If you have looked into this theory in other books you may have written it off as being difficult to understand and full of confusing terms such as azimuth, altitude and horizon. The truth is that this form of astrology is laughably easy to understand and it takes no astrological knowledge whatsoever to make use of it. As long as you have a colored computer screen to look at or colored printouts of the maps, as long as you can tell one color from another and understand the glyphs (symbols) that represent each of the planets, you will be up and running in absolutely no time at all. For example, on your Local Space Map printout, a Jupiter line is blue, a Venus line is green, and that - along with a list of the glyphs - is the total amount of scientific knowledge that you will need! I often tack a Local Space Map reading on to the end of a regular astrology reading and my clients are invariably totally fascinated with the system, if for no other reason than the fact that *they can read it for themselves!*

Altitude, horizon and azimuth

It won't be necessary for you to know what the terms, altitude, horizon and azimuth mean unless you become heavily involved in celestial navigation (navigating by the stars). However, I am a great believer in taking the mystery out of astrology, so here is my "duffers' guide" to these words, within the astrological context used in this book:

• **Altitude.** This is fairly obvious, of course, it means the height of a star or planet above the horizon.

• **Horizon.** This is the line where the sky meets the earth (forgetting about mountains and valleys, of course!). If you watch the Moon and stars at night, you will see them appear or disappear over the horizon.

• **Azimuth** is an angle; if you drop an imaginary vertical line from a planet to the horizon, and imagine another line pointing due North from you to the horizon, azimuth is the angle between these two points.

• **Altazimuth** is a measurement used in celestial navigation, calculated by a combination of a planet's altitude and azimuth. Basically, the altazimuth and horizon tell you how high and at what compass degree a planet is located.

If you use a compass to find magnetic North, then you can work out what degree a celestial object's azimuth is at any point in time.

Local Space Maps made simple

Let us for a moment go back in time to the days when sailors used the stars to navigate the seas. Imagine that you are on a ship, looking at a planet shining in the sky, and then take an imaginary line vertically down from that planet to the surface of the sea, then through the spot where you are standing and out the other side - this line will be your Local Space Map line for that planet. Local Space Map charts show this as lines on the surface of the globe, and they are drawn as at the date and time of your birth .

If you would like to do this for real, wait for a clear evening and take a look at the darkening sky just after the sun has set. The few 'stars' that begin to appear are actually planets - the stars proper don't show themselves until a little later. If you are an early bird, you can take a look at the sky just before the sun rises; the last few 'stars' that you see before they fade

away are the planets. You don't need to know which planet is
which at this stage, it is just a nice idea to pop out and look at
these objects and to get the idea of drawing an imaginary line
down towards you and through you and out the other side
again.

Now, imagine a newborn baby who just happened to be
born out of doors on a bright starlit night. This baby is so
advanced that he sits up immediately after being born, looks

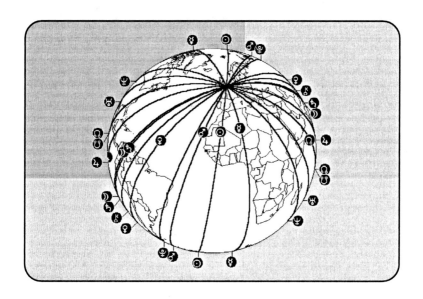

"Globe" view of a Local Space Map

around the sky, locates the planets and then draws an imaginary line from each planet down and through the spot where he is sitting, and then on behind him, all the way around the Earth. If you look at the illustration, I think you will get the idea very quickly.

So what can you use Local Space Map astrology for? Your Local Space Map chart will show the lines that pass through your place of birth and then onwards around the world. You

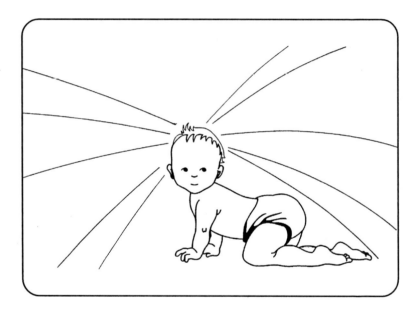

A baby's planetary lines

can use these maps in much the same way as the Astro Maps that we have described in such detail in the preceding chapters, and you don't even have to worry about what is rising, setting, on the MC or on the IC. Simply take each planetary line and read all the sections that refer to that planet. A little later in this book I will show how you can work out how these

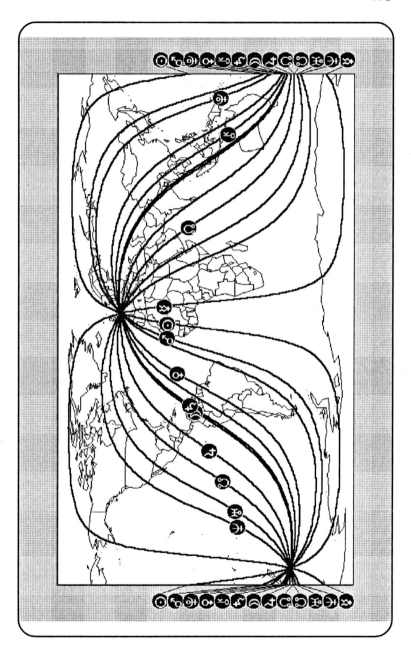

The usual view of a Local Space Map

planetary lines would affect your work, finances, home life, love life and so on, but let's keep things simple for the time being.

So, if you see that a Venus line runs towards, or near a particular location, you can be sure that this would be a pleasant place to visit or to live in. Conversely, a Saturn line would be a great place for getting down to work but not necessarily a fun place for a holiday. More to the point with this type of astrology, you can see how a journey would work out if you actually travelled along any of these lines.

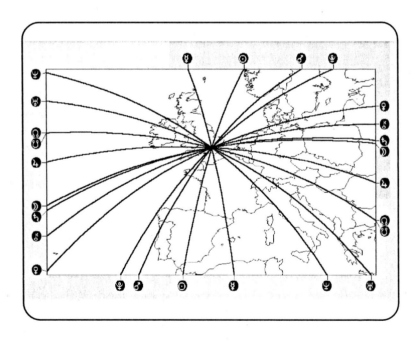

A UK map with Local Space lines on it

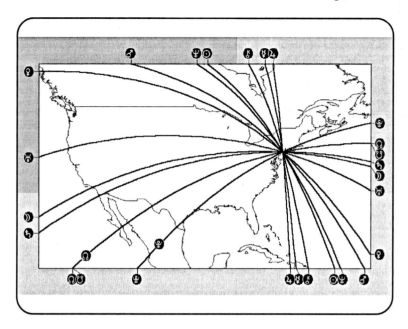

Part of the USA, showing Local Space lines

The occasional disadvantages of Local Space Maps

Some Local Space Maps views appear to compress their lines into one part of the globe, but this simply depends upon the viewpoint you are using; All the lines originate at your birthplace, or whichever other spot the map is based on, and a greater magnification of this area is needed for clarity. As the lines continue around the world, they separate, and then come together again on the opposite side of the world to your base spot.

Your computer software will enable you to make up your maps for the whole world, for a continent, a country and even quite a small part of a particular country. So if you want the 'long view', pick the kind of map that you want or switch between maps to examine your findings. However, if you want a really close up view, you can use this system as a kind of Feng Shui.

Feng Shui is a Chinese system that shows how you can arrange your house or your business for maximum luck, in this case to avoid the bad spirits and to encourage the good ones. The origins of Feng Shui are similar to those of Local Space Map Astrology, although these have been lost in the mists of time. In a moment, I will show you how you can use these maps in a very simple form of directional Feng Shui.

Your immediate locality

Print out a copy of a Local Space Map based on where you were born, magnified to show the smallest area possible around your birth place. Then trace the lines onto an overhead transparency or a sheet of tracing paper. Now you have a really handy tool at your disposal, because you can lay this down over a map of the town you were born in (make sure to align north/south correctly on both the map and tracing paper), and see how the different areas of that town affected you while you lived there. If you still live in the area, this map will still be relevant but if you have moved away, then simply make up a fresh Local Space Map using the new location and also the date and time that you moved to that location instead of using your original date, place and time of birth. Therefore, if you lost your money in Las Vegas, your handbag in Lusaka, your football boots in Singapore or your heart in Ashby-de-la-Zouch, make up your map for the date and time of your arrival in the relevant location and see what you can find! You might manage to locate your lost boots, but I'm not sure how you would go about getting your lost heart back again, though!

Local Space Maps for your premises

Copy the instructions from the previous paragraph and lay your Local Space Map lines over a rough drawing of your house, your place of work or anywhere else that interests you. Simply make up the map (or have one made up by an astrologer), and lay these lines over a rough sketch of your house, your place of work or any other place that has some special meaning for you. Remember to align north/south on both sheets first of all.

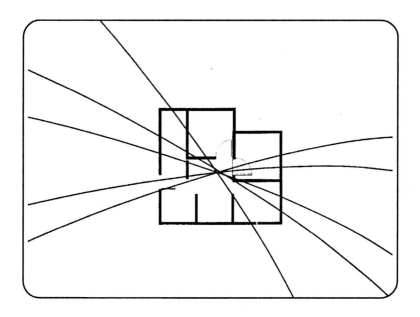

A house map

If you don't use a computer

If you are capable of making up a natal chart by hand but you don't have a computer, believe it or not, you can create a perfectly good Local Space chart by hand from your natal chart.

Start by making up a decent natal chart including Chiron and the north node, but on this occasion leave out any "extras" such as asteroids, the vertex, part of fortune, east point or anything else of the ilk. Leave the middle of the chart clear and don't put in any aspect lines. Now make several photocopies of your chart so that you have plenty to play around with. If your illustration is cramped, enlarge it. You will need a set of colored pens with fine nibs.

Start by looking at the position of the Sun on your chart and then find the exact opposite point to this on the chart. For example, if your Sun is 12 degrees of Cancer, the opposite point will be 12 degrees of Capricorn. Draw a yellow line across the chart linking these two points.

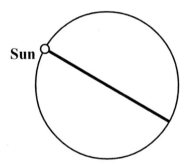

Now do the same for the Moon, using a different color; move on to do the same for all the other planets, using different colors for each one. Now go back to your instant print shop and ask them to photocopy your design on to a transparent film sheet (have a couple of copies made up in case one gets messed up while you are using it).

Now we come to the tricky part, and this will require some explanation. A normal astrological chart does not line up with what you see in an atlas. For instance, the Ascendant is supposedly in the east (where the Sun rises), but this is always found on the left-hand side of your chart. Similarly, the Midheaven should point to where the Sun shines most strongly, but this is located at the top of your chart - where the north pole would be, in an atlas, rather than pointing towards the ecliptic (the path of the Sun). If you are unclear about the astronomy or geography of this, go right back to the start of this book and review the explanation on where the Sun shines.

All astrological maps for the Northern Hemisphere are actually 180 degrees out. To make your natal chart align with any map, simply turn your page 180 degrees and your chart will now line up with east, west, north and south as does a road map, an atlas or a globe. If you were born in the Southern Hemisphere, you need to turn your chart over (literally face down) so that the Midheaven is still at the top of the chart, but with east in the east and west in the west. The reason for this chaos is that early astronomers and astrologers didn't have atlases; they didn't even know that the world was round, so they looked southwards towards the Sun and the ecliptic (the path of the Sun), and they made their charts up according to what they saw in the sky. You may have to redraw your chart to get it right for the purpose.

Once you have a workable Local Space chart on transparent film, with north actually at the top (i.e. with the IC at the top of the chart and the ascendant on the right), all you have to do is to lay this over a map of a town, village, set of buildings or your home or premises. Use a compass to work out where north is; align north on the Local Space map with north on your map.

A touch of Mundane astrology

If you enjoy experimenting a little, then the following exercise will interest you. I saw Martin Davis of Matrix UK demonstrating this and it simply amazed me. For this, you find the date and if possible the time when a particular town was 'born'. There will be a note somewhere of the date of the first meeting of the Town Council or perhaps the date when the place first became designated as a city. Then make up your map as described above and look at it. Martin demonstrated this at a talk in Leicester in the midlands of England, using the date of when Leicester became a city. From the city hall, the Pluto line led to the police station, the Neptune line to a lake that is used for leisure pursuits and the Venus line to the shopping centre.

Prime Vertical maps

As mentioned earlier, I shall now briefly tell you about the Prime Vertical and Prime Vertical maps. The Prime Vertical is a line joining the Sun's zenith to its nadir, and maps drawn using mathematical calculations based on the Prime Vertical will naturally differ from the more usual Placidus calculations. There are many different astrological house systems in use, devised for different purposes, and the Prime Vertical is the base used in the Campanus house system. The system produces unequal house spacing as in the more popular Placidus system, but there the similarity ends. There is really no point in taking you more deeply into the pros and cons of all the house systems; that would be the subject of a whole book in itself, so I will leave those of you who may be interested in the subject to look into it yourselves in your spare time.

For astrologers only - the Astrological houses

If you have one of the more sophisticated mapping computer programs, you may have become confused about the way the astrological houses seem to be arranged - if you have thought about it at all, that is! This section will demystify this for you and it will actually show you what goes on in an ordinary natal chart. In order to get to grips with this section of this book, I seriously suggest that you run off your own natal chart and those of a few friends and relatives and then photocopy them onto the kind of transparencies that are used for overhead projectors. A visit to your local print-shop will help you to achieve this. This will be an enormous help to you as it will enable you to see exactly what I am getting at. A good quality large atlas with a map of the world on it will also be invaluable to you at this point. If you don't have one of these, take your transparencies to your local library and do this exercise there using one of their super-duper atlases.

A common-or-garden natal chart for a birth in the northern hemisphere shows the ascendant on the left hand side of the chart, the descendant on the right, the MC at the top of the chart and the IC at the bottom. The houses are arranged in an anti-clockwise order starting from the ascendant. Now look at a map of the world and really think about what you are looking at, and you will immediately find that none of this makes any sense at all.

The ascendant represents the horizon where the Sun rises - but as any schoolchild will tell you, the Sun rises in the east and sets in the west. If the MC represents the highest point in the sky, where is that supposed to be? Well, for those astronomers who predated Galileo, Kepler, Copernicus and so on, the earth was flat and the top of the heavens was where the Sun shone at noon each day. In short, the top of the sky where the ecliptic runs. (The ecliptic is the apparent path of the Sun around the Earth).

Now, take your transparency birthchart, turn it upside down and place it on top of the picture of the world in the atlas with the middle of the chart dead on the place where you were born. Now the MC will be pointing south towards the ecliptic, the ascendant will point to the east, the descendant to the west and the IC to the north, away from the ecliptic and thus away from the Sun's light. Believe me, the moment you do this exercise, it will all make sense.

The situation for southern hemisphere births is different again. Sure, the ascendant must be facing east, but the MC must face north, towards the ecliptic. This time, you must turn your transparency *over* - not upside down - to put the ascendant in the east, the descendant in the west, the MC towards the ecliptic and the IC pointing away from the ecliptic.

If the term "right ascension" has ever confused you, this exercise will clear that one up too. When the right is on the right (and not on the left) the right ascension is in the right place! If you see what I mean! Again, I would like to repeat that this information is not necessary for you to understand your Astro-Map charts; it is for the benefit of all the Aquarians and the like, who want to know how things work!

Now, if you own a sophisticated mapping software program, select your own birth chart and print yourself out a globe-shaped map with the signs of the zodiac marked on it. Nothing else, just the signs. If you wish, you can erect a second chart showing the position of the Sun on your chart. You know what your Sun sign is, so the MC line for your Sun will show you exactly which part of the ecliptic this was on, at the time of your birth. If, for example, you happened to have been born when the Sun was in Capricorn, the Sun's MC line will be in the Capricorn sector of this map-chart. Do print this chart out so that you can study it for a few moments in order to absorb the idea fully. You will then notice that all the zodiac signs bisect the ecliptic at regular intervals. This is exactly how the system was worked out in ancient times. If you want further confirmation of this, get into the habit of going outside on clear nights and look at the constellations as they pass overhead, month by month, throughout the year. If you have a problem identifying the constellations, treat yourself to a couple of well-illustrated astronomy books for children.

Now print yourself out a globe map with the houses marked on it and see where they all meet. One meeting point (the important one), is at the spot where you were born. Another is opposite it on the other side of the world. Your time, date and place of birth are the starting point of your Local Space Map chart, as that is the exact point where the astrological houses are placed and from where they run around your chart. The houses also run around the globe and they also bisect the ecliptic, but not along the same "routes" as the Signs. Sit down, think about this, take a few natal charts and a few map charts, really look at them and all will become clear.

In short, to sum up, the signs of the zodiac cross the ecliptic and so do the houses, radiating like spokes from the hub of a wheel - but originating from different spots on the globe, so they go along different routes. Now you can see clearly why we as astrologers need the date, time and place where our subjects were born, in order to correctly assess their horoscopes.

You can now also note that house systems are unequal. How the different kinds of house systems have come about is another story, because some of them are mathematically arrived at, from their relationship to the celestial equator, while others refer to the celestial MC/IC line. You will be glad to know that I will not go any further into that minefield in this book. As my grandparents used to say, "Enough is enough, already!"

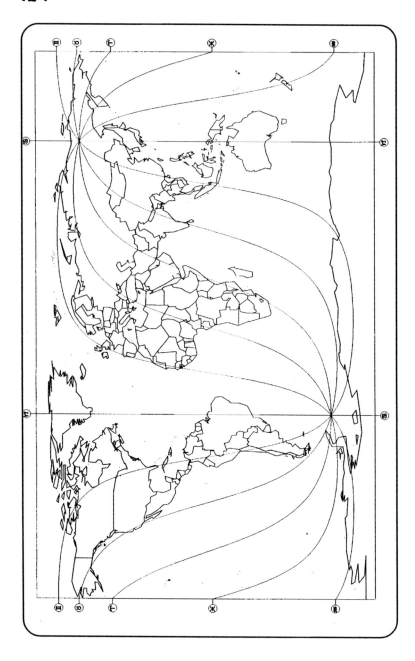

World map showing the Zodiac Signs

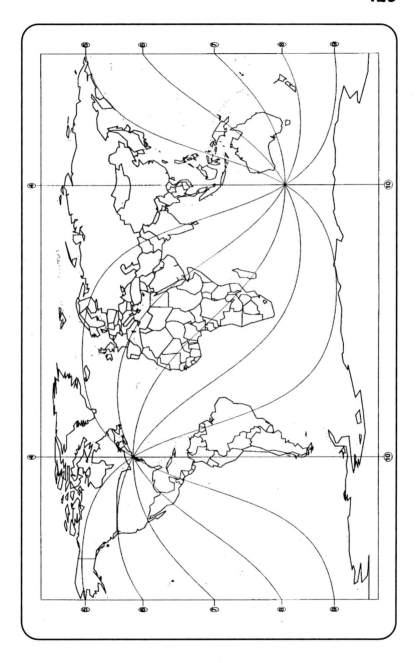

Zodiac Houses on a Local Space Map

Parans

Parans are dead easy to understand because these are simply the places where two planetary lines cross. The effect of a Paran will travel all round the world *along the line of latitude* on which the Paran is located, but the greatest force will be felt where the Paran occurs, with its effect fading away the further around the world one moves.

The effect of a Paran is much like a square aspect on an ordinary astrological chart, which suggests that the spot where the Paran is located is likely to be a particularly challenging one.

If a number of lines congregate at one particular spot, this is likely to be a very 'hot' spot and if the planets involved are difficult ones, then it might be better to avoid visiting these areas completely if you can. You (or your client) will have to be the judge of what you (or they) do or don't do during a

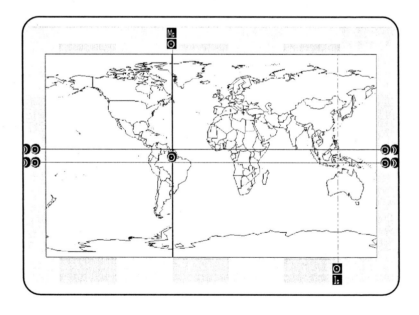

Paran lines

lifetime. For those millions of people whose jobs or whose life-styles require them to travel extensively, being aware of danger spots may be useful, but I guess that one should avoid becoming paranoid about this. I have noticed over the years that people who are new to astrology often become paranoid about a particular planet. Saturn is usually the one that they love to hate because as soon as they realize the losses, limitations and hardships that Saturn can bring, they start moaning and complaining about Saturn in their own natal charts. All planets have their good and bad points and any skilled astrologer knows that there will be ups and downs throughout life. A person who travels extensively may not be able to avoid travelling through 'bad' territories and they may have to do so at a time which is generally difficult for them. A sense of proportion and some common sense will be required here, and of course, being aware of the circumstances is half the battle.

As a personal example, I have travelled a great deal throughout my life and more often than not a major journey will occur when either Mercury or Jupiter is in retrograde motion and it is often Murphy's law that *both* of these planets are retrograde when I travel. I have come to the conclusion that this simply denotes the fact that *I am making an important journey*, and not that the journey itself will be particularly hazardous or unpleasant. Therefore, Parans should be taken as a warning that one's life will be unpredictable and unsettled while at this spot rather than as a thing to be feared. Having said all that and being my usual awkward self, I would not choose to spend any significant amount of time at a place where a number of 'nasties' happen to congregate.

Feng Shui - Move a Pot and Change your Life!

As I said in the introduction to this book, when giving talks and workshops on location astrology, I found that it was not so much the travel aspect of this that intrigued my audiences, as the idea of analyzing their own homes.

The brilliant quote at the start of this section of the book comes from a good friend of ours called Molly-Ann Fairley. Molly teaches Feng Shui at her School for Psychic Studies, and she found that some of the people who take lessons in Feng Shui may be interested in the subject for its own sake and they may even have a vague idea of becoming practitioners themselves, but the vast majority are looking for ways of improving their own lives and ridding themselves of unhappiness. In Molly's words, she once commented to Jan and me that many students aren't that interested in the math, philosophy and background to Feng Shui - what they want to do is to "move a pot and change their lives!"

This is not a book on Feng Shui, but the Local Space aspect of astrology can be used in a similar way. In this case, it is not necessarily an ornament or a plant pot that you might need to move, but yourself! Part of classic Feng Shui thinking is to keep the invisible Chi energy moving around your house in the right way, i.e. neither too quickly nor stagnating. Local Space astrology doesn't think like this; it simply shows how the planetary lines work through your home, so it isn't a case of moving something in your home in order to alter the way the energy runs, but to move yourself to a beneficial line, and to avoid a difficult one. For example, if you regularly sleep, sit or work on a difficult planetary line, you could improve your circumstances and your feelings by moving things around a little. Even if there is nothing you can move, it may help to know what is going on.

Here is a classic instance of what I mean. My previous husband, Tony, was a good deal older than I was, and deteriorating health led him to retire early from his job in engineering. After he retired, he became discontented, restless and difficult to live with. When relaxed and relatively happy, he loved to sit about, watching the television or reading book after book. His favorite armchair was situated towards the front of our house, and his favorite outdoor spot was under the apple tree in our back garden. I worked out that my own Saturn line ran right through the house and passed right through his "telly" chair at the front and his garden chair out the back - with me trying, unsuccessfully, to work in the middle. Nuff said!

Now let us assume that you have done the following:

1. You have coped with making a simple diagram of each floor of your house.
2. You have obtained, run off or hand drawn your Local Space map and photocopied it onto transparent film.
3. You have laid the film over your house diagram, using a compass to align north on the Local Space map to north on your house.
4. Let us also assume that either you know what the energies of each of the planets are, or that you have looked back through this book and used the information on each rise line to give you an idea of how they work.
5. Let us also assume that you are a glutton for punishment! Actually, to be honest, this exercise is not half as difficult to do as it may appear to be.

It is a matter of debate as to whether you use your natal Local Space chart over your home, or whether you use one for the date and time that you moved in to your home. Obviously it is best to use the chart for the time of the actual move - the time when you brought your first belongings into the new house. However, if you have lived in the same place all your life or if you can't remember exactly when you moved, you have no choice other than to transpose your Local Space chart from your actual place of birth and use it for this purpose. Put it this way, experiment with what you have and see how you get on.

You can now add the concept of the Feng Shui Magic Square to the equation. The following instructions show you how to make up this Magic Square, and what it all means. The Magic

Magic Square

Square is called "Magic" because, whichever way you add up the numbers within it, whether horizontally, vertically or diagonally, they always total 15.

Place the diagram of one floor of your house on a table, and using a pencil and ruler, draw a Magic Square over it. The numbers at the bottom (8,1,6) must be lined up with your front door. If your front door is conventionally placed at the front of your house this is easy, but if you normally use a door is at the side of the house, use that side of the house as the bottom of the Square. If you live in an apartment, use the actual door to your own apartment as the front, rather than the front door of the building that it is in.

Once you have done this with one floor of your house, do the same for the diagrams of any other floors that you may have. If the front door of the house is "cornerwise" (as in some business premises), place the bottom of the Square at the front elevation of the building. Imagine the view that people approaching the building entrance see, and put the front of the Square there.

If your house is an irregular shape, one or two sections of the Magic Square may not have a room showing in them. According to the rules of Feng Shui, you should hang a mirror on the wall of the missing part, as that will "bring" the missing part into the Magic Square. However, that doesn't help much with the system as demonstrated in this book, so you will just have to face the fact that something is missing. This alone,

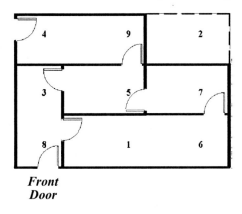

Front
Door

plus any line that runs into the missing area, will have something to say about what goes on in your home. Now treat all the other floors in your house in the same way.

Each of the numbered squares within the Magic Square refers to a specific area of your life in much the same way as do the astrological houses on a chart. In fact, the Chinese called the nine squares within the Magic Square "houses". The following list will give you a brief outline of the areas of life that these refer to:

1.   Career prospects, your self-esteem. Your potential in business and the role you play in society.

2.   Relationships of all kinds, especially marriage, partnerships and romance.

3.   The past, your ancestors and your original home. This may not mean much to Westerners, but the Chinese respect their ancestors and they often invoke their spiritual help when times are rough. This area also relates to family relationships with parents, grandparents and other older relatives - and also the prospect of inheritance.

4.   The chances of gaining and keeping wealth.

5.   Physical health and well being.

6.   This is the area where the gods and spirits are called in to help you. Friends and allies can be attracted if this area is attractive. Travel is marked here, and business travel is enhanced if this area is well treated.

7.   Children, fertility and creation. This also governs creative gifts, creative hobbies and productive use of leisure time.

8.   Education, knowledge and openness to new ideas. This brings new ideas into your life and if you need to spend time thinking, this is the place to do it.

9.   Fame, reputation and recognition. On a more mundane level, this rules the way you are viewed or esteemed by others, and the amount of respect that you win.

4 – Prosperity	9 – Recognition	2 – Relationships
3 – Parents, etc.	5 – Health	7 – Children
8 – Study	1 – Career	6 – Friends

A very basic view of the Magic Square

Now align the Local Space map over each floor of your house in turn, aligning the top of the map to north. Let us take a brief look at a few of the effects that you will ascertain from this exercise by looking at each section or house in the Magic Square. I can't go into every possibility in a book of this size, but the following should give you some idea of the way things would work. This is really a case of synthesizing the energies of the planets with the ideas contained within each segment of the Magic Square, much in the same way that a skilled astrologer synthesizes the planets, signs and houses on a natal chart. In some cases, two planets will be in the same area of the house. For this to occur, the planets would be in conjunction in the natal chart, so it becomes even more interesting to see how these blend or fight with each other in this Feng Shui / Local Space system.

Magic Square

1. Career prospects, your self-esteem. Your potential in business and the role you play in society. This is quite a good place to have a Saturn line, as the square links well with the nature of this planet. A Venus line might make your work enjoyable, but you might not strive very hard, while a Sun line would help you to achieve business goals or to make a success of yourself. Jupiter could help you to expand a career, but this might take off a little too quickly for comfort. Venus or Sun lines would enhance your self-esteem.

2. Relationships of all kinds, especially marriage, partnerships and romance. Obviously a Venus line here would enhance this area of your life, while a Mars or Pluto line would bring passion. Mercury would ensure plenty of communication between you and your partner.

3. The past, your ancestors and your original home or your home country. This area also relates to family relationships with parents, grandparents, other older relatives and the prospect of inheritance. The best line here would be the Moon line, while even Saturn might not be a bad one. Mercury would help with family communication, while Jupiter might take the family travelling - or bring it luck. The north node would ensure karmic benefits, but the south node could be a bit of a karmic drain.

4. The chances of gaining and keeping wealth. Jupiter, Venus or Mercury would be good lines to have here, but Pluto might be even better, as this can bring great wealth through involvement with other people and their funds. Saturn would bring wealth through hard work, as might Mars.

5. Physical health and well being. All the lines converge here, so every aspect of your life should be looked at and taken into consideration in a holistic manner. The middle area of your home should, ideally, be kept open and free from clutter.

6. This is the area where the gods and spirits are called in to help you. Friends and allies can be attracted if this area is attractive. Travel is marked here, especially if linked with business. This is the prime area for a Jupiter line, and Neptune could be beneficial, as could Uranus.

Chiron could be helpful here, due to the karmic lessons that can be learned from this planet, but the best feature would be the north node, as this would definitely bring karmic benefits, while the south node might drain these away.

7. Children, fertility and creation. This also governs creative gifts, creative hobbies and productive use of leisure time. This area links with the Sun, although Mercury and Venus would be quite nice too. Mars or Jupiter are useful, if you are interested in competitive games and sports.

8. Education, knowledge and openness to new ideas. This brings new ideas into your life, and if you need to spend time thinking, this is the place to do it. Mercury, Jupiter, Saturn, Uranus and Chiron all have connections with education or information technology in one form or another.

9. Fame, reputation and recognition. On a more mundane level, this rules the way you are viewed or esteemed by others, and the amount of respect that you win. Venus rules self-esteem, the Sun and Saturn rule esteem by others. The Sun and Jupiter can rule fame and fortune, so these are the best planets for this area.

So, what can you do to improve matters?

Ignoring the Local Space astrology factor for the moment, you could buy one of the many books on Feng Shui and use the "cures" to improve the Chi energy in and around your house, thus eliminating the negative and stimulating the positive energies. However, if you look at the way you use your home, perhaps there is something you can change in order to tap into the beneficial aspects of the Local Space astrology and eliminate some of the negatives.

You might be able to change the door you normally use to enter the house for one that "lets in" a more favorable planet. If you are lucky enough to have the kind of space that allows you to change rooms from one use to another, perhaps you could do that. It would be difficult to swap a kitchen for a bedroom, but you might be able to turn a bedroom into a study or sitting room, or vice versa. If you can't make major alterations, you might be able to swap the room you sleep in for a different bedroom, leaving the less favorable room for occasional guests, even if the room you move out of is larger or nicer. You may have a sitting room and a dining room which would work better the other way around.

Take a look at the seat you regularly use; is this on a Saturn or a Pluto line? If so, you could feel quite uncomfortable or even unwell on that spot, while simply moving the seat from one side of the room to another would make you feel better. If you work from home and you find it difficult to discipline yourself and to get down to things, find the Saturn line and move your worktable and tools or equipment to that area. The following planetary list shows a few further ideas that might be worth consideration.

The **Sun** line, whether inside the house or close to it, is great for fun, for playing with children, for knockabout games or for playing at cards and board games, for leisure, relaxing or spending time with your partner.

The **Moon** line is wonderful for preparing or eating food, or for family gatherings, and this can happen indoors or on a patio or barbecue.

A **Mercury** line is terrific for telephoning friends, writing letters, working on a computer or planning a sales campaign; also for short bursts of study or work.

A **Venus** line, whether indoors or outside, is great for lovemaking, relaxation, eating, drinking with friends and working on any kind of hobby or interest that involves creating something attractive. This is also a good planet for a greenhouse or a garden area that you enjoy working in or sitting around in.

Mars is the energy planet, so, if you play sports close to your home, or if you take exercise inside it, try to do this on a Mars line. If you work from home and you need extra energy, situate your work area on this line. Sex could be hot and exciting on a Mars line.

Jupiter is wonderful for educational or spiritual matters, so if you need to study, do this on a Jupiter line. If you like to keep or read books on spiritual matters, place them around a Jupiter line.

The **Saturn** line will help you to keep your nose to the grindstone, so either place a home-study area around this line or at worst keep your brooms, brushes and washing machine or utility room on this line.

Uranus is a strange planet, and most astrology books will tell you that it causes unpredictable or unexpected events - and it can do just that. However, Uranus rules democracy and group activities, where one person's ego is submerged by the needs of the group. Therefore, if you enjoy family discussions or group decisions, perhaps you could do this on your household Uranus line. This is a good area for sitting around with friends, or for trying out anything inventive or original.

The **Neptune** area is ideal for your bath or shower room. If you enjoy relaxing in the bath with a panoply of essences, concoctions and candles throwing a soft light, then the Neptune line can only enhance this. Otherwise, it is all right for a bedroom or any other place that you relax in. If you can afford to build a swimming pool, choose a Neptune line.

The **Pluto** line is probably best used for love making, as this will increase your passion quotient. This is a great place for working out your savings plans, mortgage, taxes and other official money matters. If you wish to transform yourself or your life, sit down on your Pluto line and decide to change the way you dress, the color of your hair, your car, your job, your lover, your attitudes - and if all else fails - plan your next house-move!

Progressions, Transits, and more...

Progressions and transits will only make sense to reasonably serious astrologers, so if this means nothing to you, leave it for now and come back to it when you get further into astrology.

If your software allows you to superimpose a progressed or transit chart over a natal one, you will notice that on a world map, the lines are too numerous and too confusing to read. If you print out or keep a copy of your natal Astro-Map or Local Space Map chart by your computer and then zoom in to a smaller area, you will soon see the details far more easily, and it will become much clearer to you.

You can then try progressing your natal chart from the *natal location,* or moving to a new location and *then* progressing your chart. The name of the game here is to experiment with as many charts as you can, and to ask a few "guinea pigs" with whose maps you are playing, what happened to them when they relocated to their new homes, or what was the outcome of any business dealings that are attached to a specific location.

When doing ordinary astrology, a decent astrologer will always relocate a progressed chart to a new location, so why not do so when progressing any of the Map charts? If a specific period of time is of interest to the astrologer or his client, then a transit chart is also worth looking at. Transit charts show a particular moment in time, and thus they are of particular interest to someone who is doing business in a different location at a specific point in time. The same can be said for someone who wants to know how a holiday or visit to friends in a different location will turn out.

Research possibilities

So many famous people have had life changing experiences while on the move or while spending time at a specific location, and it poses the question that if they had not gone to that particular place or had they not chosen to become closely identified with a particular location, would their lives have been easier, harder, more ordinary or just different? Locational astrologers all seem to have homed in on President Kennedy and Dallas, but there are so many other historic and celebrity figures that can be considered. For example, Scott of the Antarctic, Clive of India, Anthony Eden and Suez, Cecil Rhodes and Kimberley, Paul Hogan and Hollywood, Oskar Schindler and Krakow, Berlin, Brinnlitz and Vicente in the Argentine, or finally poor Princess Diana and Paris, and my own story of meeting my present husband while 6,000 miles away from my home.

Eclipse paths

If you buy a program that shows the paths of the eclipses, you may want to try out an idea that was suggested to me by my friend, Sean Lovatt. Call up the nearest eclipse before a person's birth and see where the path of this goes, and then see what this means to the person in question. In Hitler's chart, the eclipse path ends at El Alamein.

In the following map, the figures on the lines on either side of the direct eclipse path are decimals. Thus, where the eclipse is total, you'll see the number 100. As one moves away from the direct path of the eclipse, its visibility drops down through 0.75, 0.5 and 0.25 to zero visibility.

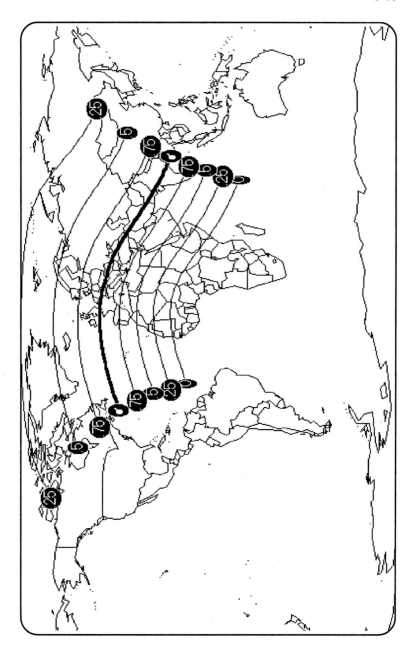

Eclipse path

Other Forms of Relocated Chart

Astro-Geodetics

If you know enough about astrology to spot the MC on an ordinary natal chart, then you will find it very easy to understand Astro-Geodetics, and you don't need a computer for this. Your starting point is a common-or-garden natal chart.

If you can remember back to your school days, you will know that a circle is divided into 360 degrees. If you take a look at the world map in an ordinary school atlas, you will see that this is divided into twelve equal longitudinal segments of thirty degrees. These twelve segments correspond to the thirty-degree segments of the zodiac, starting at Greenwich, which corresponds to 0 deg. Aries.

Now if you move towards the west, each degree that you travel will move the MC on your chart *forward* by one degree, and if you move towards the east, each degree that you travel will move the MC *backwards* by one degree. The latitude is of no importance in this technique, you only need to take the longitude into consideration.

Here is a tip that will help you to remember the theory and it comes from two navigators, one being my work partner, Sean Lovatt, who has his own boat, and from my own experience as a private pilot. *East is least and west is best!* Meaning that the MC increments *upwards* through the zodiac to the west, and downwards through the zodiac to the east.

So, if you were born in London, England, and your MC is 17 deg. Libra and you move to Cape Town, your new MC will move back by roughly one sign to become 17 deg. Virgo. If you move to Miami, the MC will move roughly forward four signs to become 17 deg. Aquarius. This is a rough and ready explanation, but a glance at an atlas will make it clear.

The next step is to make up a natal chart with the new MC and then to see how the planets fit the new pattern. If you have software that allows you to rectify a chart on the screen, this is a simple matter. If not, just make a new chart up by hand by locating the new MC in the Raphael's Ephemeris and then looking up the new ascendant and the houses in the old-fashioned way. You can, of course, experiment with progressed Astro-geodetic charts as well as relocated natal charts.

It would be nice to be able to say that all you need to do is to make up a chart as if the person had been born in the different location, i.e. setting the place of birth for London in England rather than New York in the USA, but that doesn't work. The only way is to move the MC and then move everything else. It is probably also worth using an Equal House chart to simplify matters.

The end result of this is that you have basically the same birthchart, with all the planets in the same place in the same signs as in the natal chart, but the angles will have changed. The angles are the Ascendant (Asc), Descendant (Dsc), Midheaven (Medium Coeli / MC) and Immum Coeli (IC). Also, the houses will be different. Planets that were in the seventh house of relationships may now be in the sixth or eighth houses, or planets that were in the twelfth may now be in the first or the eleventh houses.

For those of you who are interested in Mundane astrology, you might like to take a look at the charts of the cities and countries that you are travelling to (and away from), and see if there is anything there that links with your own natal or Astro-Geodetic charts.

All this sounds rather complicated, and it can be, but the following letter shows how interesting this kind of chart can be, just by looking around to see what is close to the new MC.

A look at the new Asc, Dsc, IC and other features would be even more interesting.

Astro-Geodetics in action

I would like to pass on to you the contents of an email which was sent to me by a German astrologer called Karin, who tested out the Astro-Geodetics system on her own chart and also those of her children.

" I tested the information you sent me about the MC moving from Greenwich to east or west, and I thought you might be interested in my findings. My intuitive Scorpio/Pisces son has always had a strong attraction to Asia and has actually taken courses in the Japanese language. He recently managed to be sent to Tokyo by his US company for two years, and he is very happy there. His Scorpio Sun sits on the MC when he is in Tokyo. My daughter has very successfully graduated from London University College and now has an M. Phil from King's College in London. Her MC there is conjunct her 29 degrees Pisces Sun and is one degree away from her Jupiter. My own attraction to San Francisco and the film world in Los Angeles seems to be explained by my three Leo planets, plus my north node falling into the 10th house with the Astro-geodetic MC around 29 degrees Cancer. Amazing! After so many years, astrology continues to fill me with awe..."

Progressed or transit Astro-Geodetic charts

Naturally, you can combine your Astro-Geodetic chart with progressions and transits in any combination that you fancy experimenting with.

Progressed charts

All your usual forms of progressed charts, that is day-for-a-year charts (also known as secondary directions), Solar arc charts and Solar and Lunar return charts can and indeed *should* be relocated. So if you are thinking of moving to another location, progress your chart by whatever method you prefer to use and look at the situation in your new location. You will notice that the ascendant and MC move quite a bit if a major journey is undertaken and in some cases, this movement can put the new ascendant back into the twelfth house of the original natal chart. Try my favorite method of secondary directions (day-for-a-year Progressions) and see what happens to the new chart.

If your computer program offers you a choice of precessed charts, it is a matter of personal preference as to whether you use these or not.

A final word

Locational astrology has been around for centuries but it is only the advent of modern computer programs that allows ordinary folk to understand and to use it. This is the first book that makes these methods accessible to ordinary astrologers. Research astrologers and theorists have tried to find their way around these techniques but the ground roots knowledge and experience of working astrologers has yet to develop. It is *your* use of this book and the systems that are described in it that will bring about the coming explosion in knowledge.

The Astro-Map charts are great if you are thinking of travelling or of doing business in a part of the world that is at a distance from your place of birth. These give a wonderful world view which can be pared down to allow you to home in on a new location anywhere else in the world.

The Local Space Maps can be used for world travel, but they are even better for use in single countries, states or provinces or for local area, domestic and workplace Feng Shui.

Astro-Geodetics is interesting to play with, but it can't really be assessed for its usefulness until more astrologers use it.

Remember that all the normal forms of progressed and return charts should be relocated to the place where you were, are or will be at the time in question.

So what about interplanetary travel?

I dread to think of how astrologers will cope with births on other planets, or worse still, on space ships travelling around the universe! I don't usually shrink from a challenge, but I have to say that I am glad that both the computing that creates these charts, and interpreting them will be some future astrologer's problem, not mine! Astrology has been around for millennia. Along with medicine, prostitution and finding enough food for the family, this is probably one of the oldest jobs around, and like these, it will doubtless still be around when the Sun and the Earth grow old, despite those astronomers and scientists who insist that it is bunkum.

So, whether you are new to astrology and not really able to make up or interpret charts as a whole, or whether you are as steeped in it as I am, use my book to enjoy your location astrology or to see what is right or wrong with your home or your business premises.

The Systems in Action...

The systems in action: Oskar Schindler

Many people find case histories useful; for those of you who like them, I thought it would be useful to include a couple here, using a combination of Astro-Map and Local Space techniques. I chose to illustrate Oskar Schindler's life story as one example because it is so well known and also so extraordinary. Oskar Schindler was born on 28 April 1908 at 21:29 hours CET, near Prague, in what is now the Czech Republic. He was actually born just outside Prague, but this location will work perfectly well. Schindler's time of birth is not recorded, but I am a dab hand at rectification, so I would be very surprised if the natal chart overleaf that I have come up with has much wrong with it.

Oskar Schindler was born into a comfortable middle class family, and by all accounts, he and his sister had a happy childhood. During his teens and early twenties, Oskar became an amateur racing driver, winning a couple of important races in Germany. Papa Schindler was a hard worker, but he loved the good things in life, and to the chagrin of his straitlaced wife, he was also a womanizer. The Schindler family were Sudeten Germans, so when the Second World War started, they were in a privileged position in Czech society. Oskar liked to live well and to enjoy himself, but he wanted to do this without making too much physical effort. Although pretty amoral and a badge-wearing member of the Nazi party, Oskar was not a Nazi fanatic and he had absolutely no intention of joining the German armed forces, nor putting up with any

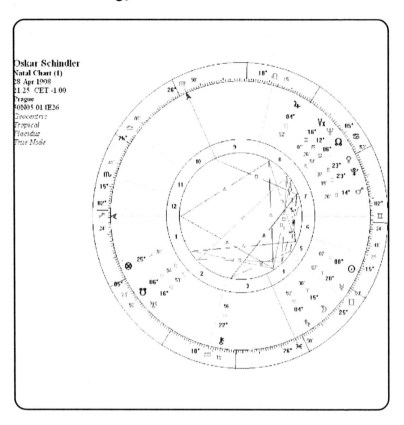

Oskar Schindler: natal chart

undue discomfort for the cause. Oskar looked around for a way of keeping in with the Nazis, keeping himself out of trouble and getting rich. His first excursion into wartime financial activities was linked, amazingly, to the actual trigger that fired the first shot in the Second World War.

The Nazi invasion of Poland in September 1939 began with a nasty little plot. Hitler arranged for some German convicts to be dressed in Polish uniforms and armed with Polish guns and explosives. These men were killed and posthumously accused of blowing up a German radio transmitter just inside the German/Polish border. The Poles were declared to have perpetrated this "outrage", thus giving Hitler the excuse for invading their country. This bright idea was an exact copy of the Mukden incident in Manchuria in 1931, which the Japanese used as an excuse to invade China. Guess who found the Polish uniforms and side arms for this dirty little job? It was Mr. Fix-it himself, Oskar Schindler! It is unlikely, however, that he was aware of the intended purpose for the unusual order of Polish equipment.

As the war progressed and before the dreaded call-up (draft) papers arrived, Oskar looked for a business that would supply essential goods to the German armed forces. Whether he deliberately avoided anything that involved making armaments or not is unknown, but in the event, he found what he needed in the shape of a rundown enamelware factory on the outskirts of Cracow in Poland. Despite the fact that the war was already underway, Oskar borrowed the start-up money from a couple of local Jewish businessmen. Early in 1940, he changed the name of the business from its original Jewish/Polish one to the Deutsche Emailwaren Fabrik, and once his workers were installed, the factory became known by the popular name of "Emalia". Emalia started to turn out enamel pots, pans and crockery for the armed forces. At this point, Oskar had no particular love for Jews, but no particular dislike for them either. He chose to employ more Jews than Poles in his factory for a very practical reason; the local Nazis extracted payment for each worker that was employed, but Poles needed to be paid a small wage in addition, while Jewish workers didn't. Unusually for a German boss in those strange days, Oskar did not beat, bully or kill any of his workers, and he even saw to it that the children were properly trained for the work and looked after as well as could be expected under the circumstances. Oskar didn't have the instincts of a social worker. His workers themselves knew the consequences of not making an effort and they didn't need to be driven, so he didn't bother to do so.

It appears that he took no pleasure in hurting others unnecessarily, so he simply didn't do it. Oskar was all for doing those things that did give him pleasure, like eating, drinking and making love with pretty women.

Oskar became disgusted at the greedy and gross behavior of his German overlords, while at the same time coming to respect the starkly contrasting attitudes and the morality of the Jews who worked for him. The major turning point came when Oskar and one of his girlfriends were out horse riding on the hills above Cracow. By chance this happened to be the week in which Amon Goeth, the local Gauleiter, cleared the Cracow Ghetto of its Jews. The sight of the Nazis and their dogs rounding up these people as though they were vermin disturbed Oskar.

Eventually, Oskar's workers were moved to a concentration camp at Plasow, but they spent their days away from the camp and working at "Emalia". Many Jews died at the camp, but none died at Oskar's hands or in his factory. At one point, he discovered that some of "his" women and children had been sent to Auschwitz in error. This high handed behavior on behalf of some little official with a tick-list angered him so much that he showed great courage and enterprise by going to Auschwitz himself and demanding that his "skilled workers" be handed back to him. He could have left them to their fate and found other workers, but by this time, he knew each of his employees personally and he had a sense of paternal ownership towards them.

When the fortunes of war swung totally away from the Nazis, Oskar paid for the Cracow factory to be dismantled, building a new one at Brinnlitz in Czechoslovakia at his own expense, and moving all 1,200 of his workers there. This factory was directed to make shells and armaments, but Oskar and his workers ensured that the factory never turned out any useful weaponry. This way, Oskar avoided supporting a regime that he had come to loathe, while at the same time ensuring that he would be looked upon benevolently by those who took over in Europe when the war was over.

After the war, Oskar tried farming in Vicente Lopez, near Buenos Aires in Argentina. He failed in this venture, and others. Always a heavy drinker, he began to drink himself to death. Oskar drifted around Austria, Germany and even Israel, but he usually returned to South America. For much of his later life, he was supported by pensions from friends in Israel. Oskar died in poverty in South America, but his body was taken to the Mount of Olives in Jerusalem. A tree was planted in the Avenue of Righteous Nations and a plaque placed at its base. Oskar would have loved the fame, honor and love that have been so rightly awarded to him since his death. He would have been thrilled by the books and the film about him. For the most part, Oskar Schindler's life was a complete waste and a trial to many people, but his spectacular wartime behavior whisked him into immortality and universal love.

The story of the maps

Taking chart 1 first, there is little to see in Europe in Schindler's basic Astro-Map chart. The closest line to Israel is the Moon IC line, which shows that his eventual burial in Israel was a form of homecoming.

The most interesting is chart 2, the one showing Vicente in Argentina, which is bracketed by the Neptune MC and Moon DC lines. On one hand, Neptune on the Midheaven can mean living a deeply religious life or having the kind of social conscience that leads to sacrificing one's own needs entirely for those of others. The other interpretation is of a life that is thrown away or lost in drink or drugs. This was the only part of the world that Oskar actually chose to live in; all the others were dictated by fate or by other people.

Having said that, a look a the Parans shows a few interesting facts. The Moon/Mercury Paran passes through Berlin and three Parans all run through southern Poland and northern

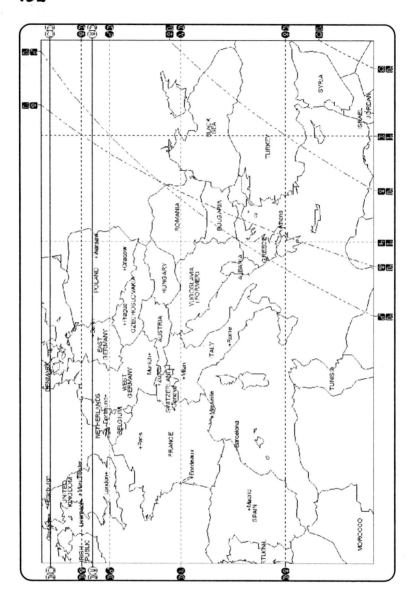

Oskar Schindler, chart 1: Astro-Map

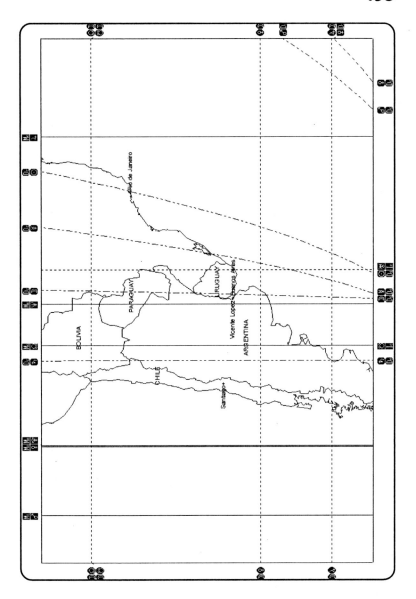

Oskar Schindler, chart 2: Astro-Map

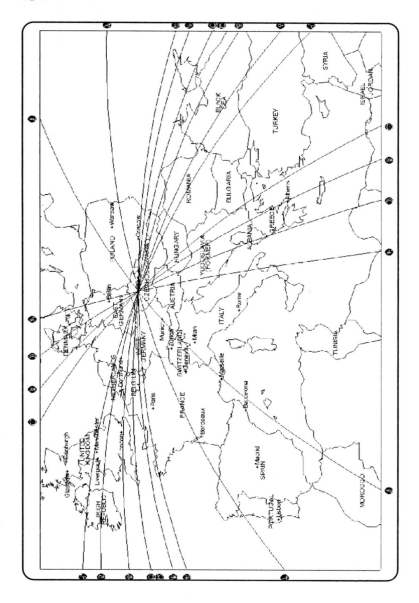

Oskar Schindler, chart 3: Local Space Map

Czechoslovakia - these being Sun/Chiron, Jupiter/Chiron and Sun/Uranus. The combination of Sun, Chiron, Jupiter and Uranus all running through one area suggests an immense force for change, enlightenment, discovery of something to believe in, self-discovery and an understanding of the nature of suffering - albeit in this case, the suffering of others rather than Oskar himself.

When we look at Oskar's natal Local Space Map (chart 3), it really brings the story to life. Saturn rules restrictions, responsibility and hardship, but also deep and enduring foundations and structures, status, respect and the achievement of ambitions through hard work. It is also the planet that rules the Jewish race. Oskar's Local Space Map shows the Saturn line running north from where he was born, past Berlin, showing where the architects of his unlikely fate were based. The Jupiter line runs close to Cracow, suggesting luck, education and discovering a set of beliefs, and even the fact that he spent a lot of time riding horses for pleasure while there. The Uranus and Neptune lines run through Brinnlitz. In this case, Neptune brought sacrifice for a higher cause - along with his usual boozing and womanizing. Building the factory in Brinnlitz, bribing his way to get permission for his workers to be moved there, and keeping them safe took every penny of the spectacular fortune that Oskar had made during the war years. Uranus is indicative of his sudden and unexpected decision to save "his" people and for the group as a whole to benefit. The nearest planet to Israel on this chart is the Sun, which demonstrates the fame, esteem and love that he has inspired. Saturn rules trees, and Oskar's only monument is the tree in the Avenue of Righteous Nations. Oskar spent a lifetime avoiding Saturnian discipline, but in the end it is the Saturn images of a tree, a plaque and a grave in a Jewish cemetery that became his monuments.

The Systems in Action: President George W. Bush and the terrorist attacks in the USA

At the time of writing this piece, just two weeks have passed since the terrorist attacks of 11 September 2001 on New York and Washington. These terrible, incomprehensibly cruel acts will be indelibly scarred in people's memories, and it has been impossible to think of anything else for any length of time. I needed to try to understand what had happened, and why; if only to ease my mind. I usually look to astrology in the first instance when assimilating something difficult, and this is what I did in this instance. As the days passed, I thought of looking at an Astro-Map for George Bush, whose chart details are readily available. His chart should be very accurate, because American birth certificates note the time of a person's birth.

Usama (Osama) Bin Laden is a different matter. In days gone by when I worked as a consultant astrologer and palmist, I would read the hands of any Arab clients that came my way, but I never tried to use astrology due to the lack of accurate birth data. I know that Interpol and others have posted a birth date for Usama Bin Laden, and there is even a birth time quoted by one astrologer. There is obviously a date on his passport, but despite all this "evidence" I am not convinced as to the accuracy of his natal details, and there are a number of sources which present conflicting data, even as far as his year of birth is concerned.

Some Arab parents in Saudi keep a note of a child's date by their religious calendar, but often the mother is very young and perhaps even illiterate. The sons of wealthy Arabs are often separated from their mothers at around eight or nine years of age and packed off to religious institutions. An Arab is allowed four wives at a time and divorce is easy, so if he can afford to do so, an Arab man will marry many times and have many children. In Bin Laden's case, his father has had many wives and apparently 57 children, so this patriarch may not even remember the names of some of his offspring, let alone their birth data. In the circumstances, there is no point in trying to construct an Astro-Map, for which the time of birth is such an important factor.

President George W. Bush

President Bush's maps show the story surrounding the attack quite clearly. If one didn't know better, one might assume at first sight that these were the Astro-Maps of a terrorist who planned and carried out these atrocious acts. However, what we are seeing here is actually a "reflection situation", which occurs when a subject is on the *receiving* end of certain acts, rather than performing them himself. One sees the same kind of thing on the charts of those who experience violence in relationships, major theft, swindles and so forth.

President Bush was born in Connecticut with Mercury and Pluto close to the Ascendant on his birth chart, so the proximity to Boston and New York would suggest that these two planets' rise lines appear in those areas - and they do. In chart 1, President Bush's Mercury rise line is close to Boston (the place from which the terrorists' planes took off), while his Pluto rise line crosses Manhattan. Mercury is associated with local travel rather than overseas travel. Pluto is noted for conspiratorial activities that are planned in secret for a long time before they see the light of day. Pluto was the king of the underworld and also the richest of the Roman gods, so he quite neatly represents the very well-to-do Usama Bin Laden and the terrorist conspiracy on President Bush's chart.

Jupiter and the Moon move to the IC close to Washington. The Moon emphasizes the fact that this is George Bush's heartland, and Jupiter suggests an increase of patriotism and fellow feeling in the USA, in addition to foreign and spiritual matters. Fairly close to Pittsburgh, Chiron moves to the IC, which suggests that lessons may be learned from the deaths of the passengers in the plane that came down there. It appears that the black box, which has been retrieved from that flight,

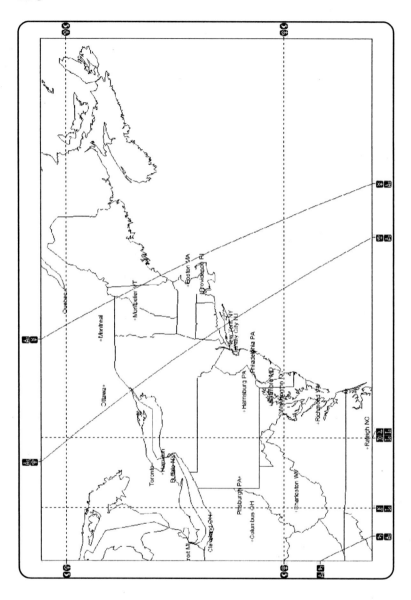

President George W. Bush - chart 1: Astro-Map

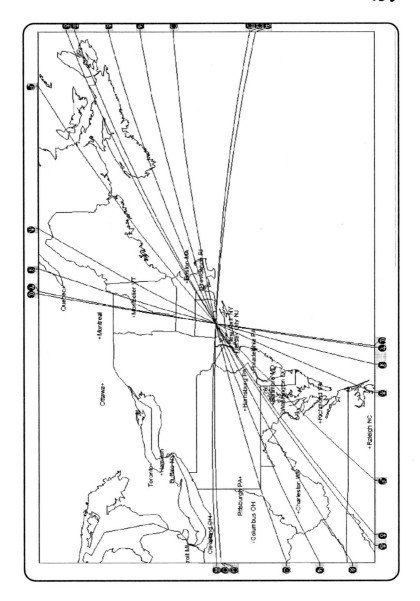

President George W. Bush - chart 2: Local Space Map

has indeed revealed some important facts (not yet disclosed at the time of writing).

At first I could find no Parans significantly close to either New York or Washington, but then I decided to look a bit wider, and I discovered that the Paran of a body called The Black Moon, or Lilith, runs right by the Washington / Pentagon area. I haven't discussed asteroids in this book, and it is arguable that this particular mass of material is little more than a collection of boulders and gas. Nevertheless, I felt inclined to include this data, because my researches have shown me that Lilith (as I call this body) has a very nasty effect on ordinary natal charts when it is activated by transits. Lilith seems to have a destructive nature that is similar to Kali in Hindu mythology.

When using the Local Space system (chart 2), the proximity of President Bush's birth to the city of New York means that many Local Space lines cross this area, with Mars (the bringer of war), Venus (open enemies) and Pluto (secret attacks) passing practically through what were the World Trade Center buildings. These lines then move on to bracket Washington and the Pentagon.

When we look at the Afghanistan portion of chart 3, Mars rises to President Bush's Midheaven and passes by Kandahar (one of Usama Bin Laden's hangouts). There are several Parans. As my software only handles one Paran at a time, I have included three separate maps. The first map (chart 3) shows Lilith crossing Venus in two areas, the first close by the capital, Kabul, and the second bordering Pakistan. Lilith also makes a Paran to Mars just to the north of Kandahar.

The next illustration (chart 4) shows an upper Paran of Neptune crossed by Uranus in the north of Afghanistan. This combination suggests sudden explosive events (Uranus) regarding a matter of religion or spiritual belief, hatched in a place of seclusion (Neptune). The lower Paran of Neptune crosses the line of the north and south nodes of the Moon. The

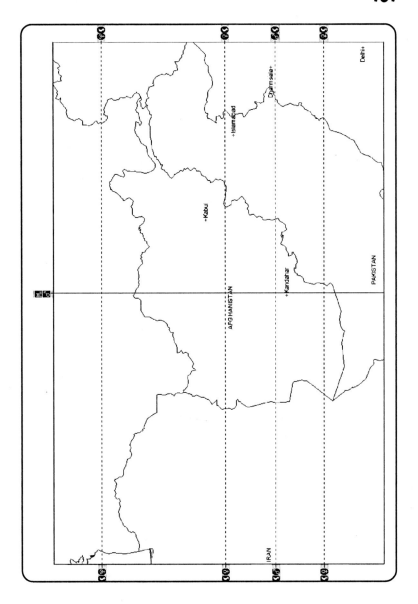

President George W. Bush - chart 3: Astro-Map

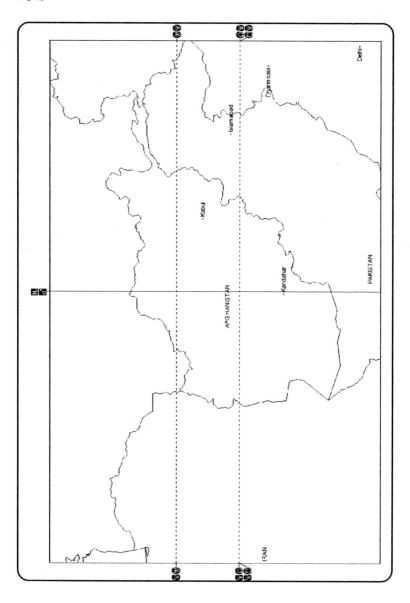

President George W. Bush - chart 4: Astro-Map

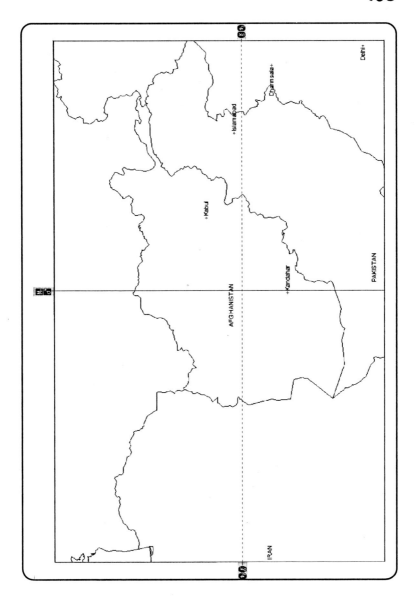

President George W. Bush - chart 5: Astro-Map

nodes are said to deal with matters of karma, also political, career or social events that are not entirely under a person's control.

The last Paran map (chart 5) shows a Saturn/Chiron Paran crossing the middle of Afghanistan. This Paran almost brushes Islamabad, the capital of Pakistan, while travelling not far south of Kabul, the capital of Afghanistan.

Finally...

I tried a Local Space map for the Afghanistan area, but nothing of apparent significance showed up. This is not unexpected, as Local Space maps leave out great swathes of the earth's surface, and it is really better to use these for local rather than global matters.

Nevertheless, it will be interesting to see, as events unfold, whether any future events disclose further connections to Astro-Map features shown here. If so, I will include developments in future editions of this book. In the meantime, although the correlations discussed above are intriguing, I still have no satisfactory answer to the question "Why?" that is lodged in my mind.

The systems in Action: A Love Story

As a nice change from the previous two case histories, here is a true love story of the kind that usually one only encounters between the pages of a romantic novel. The lovers in question are my second husband, Jan Budkowski and I.

Back in 1988, my publishers sent me on a promotional tour of South Africa, starting from Johannesburg. This visit led me to fall in love with that beautiful country. During the course of that trip, I developed a firm friendship with Vivien Watchorn, who had been co-opted to look after me; I also became close to her family. After my return, Vivien and I remained in contact and we occasionally discussed the possibility of arranging a return trip, complete with lectures and seminars. Eight years sped by before this came off, and by then, my first marriage had deteriorated to the point of no return, and I was in a pretty depressed state. I knew both personally and astrologically that I was almost on the point of doing something radically different with my life, but even I could not have predicted the turn of events that followed.

Radio 702 is Jo'burg's favorite radio station, but Saturday evening is a poor time for radio, so 702 filled in this spot with a two-hour astrology phone-in program. One Saturday evening during my trip, I was invited to join the resident astrologer on the program. For some strange reason, she wasn't in the mood to work, so she gladly handed the program over to me.

Around 15 minutes into program, a local banker, Jan Budkowski, got into his car to drive home after visiting friends. Being an amateur astrologer, he automatically reached out and turned the knob on his radio to tune into the weekly astrology program. This knob might just as well have been a Wheel of Fortune - and it began to spin furiously! He was intrigued to find that instead of the usual South African astrologer, someone with an obviously English accent had taken over. He soon realized that he was listening to the author of several of the books that he kept on his bookshelf.

During the next hour, Jan found himself filled with a weird, inexplicable and urgent desire to meet me, and he also felt that he "knew" that I had an exceptionally good soul. When I announced that I was doing a day's seminar the following week, he decided that if he had to move heaven and earth, he would be there.

Several hours before the seminar started, the skies had opened and the dirt roads around Johannesburg became dangerously flooded. Only five people made it through the floods, including Jan, who had practically taken his life in his hands to be there, travelling from some distance north of Jo'burg. By the time we stopped for mid-morning coffee, he knew that he must find some way of getting closer to me, and by the time we stopped for lunch, he knew that he wanted to marry me.

After my return to London, we kept in touch and over the following weeks, my life took a strange turn. My hitherto secure job disappeared, my children moved away or had no special need of me, my aged mother died and a number of other disasters crowded in, all at the same time. My normal life just didn't exist any more. Realizing that there was nothing to keep me in the house, I moved out to stay with a friend. I phoned Jan later that day and the next day he caught a plane to London. A week later we both left for South Africa.

Shortly after that, we took a trip north to Zambia, and temporarily sct up our first home together in a tent on the north bank of the Zambezi River - hence the name of our publishing business. We saw a fair bit of Southern Africa and then rented an apartment in Jo'burg. Jan's previously comfortable banking career had also fallen apart and the lack of any new work opportunities for Jan and the distance from all my contacts meant that we had to leave. We settled in London, where we were married, not long after all these major changes and events that were first triggered in Jo'burg. After much deliberation, we threw our last savings into a publishing business. Four years later, Jan and I moved to Plymouth, where we are now happily living and working in the world of publishing. No-one could have predicted exactly how our lives were to change so radically, and so swiftly!

My Astro-Map shows the Mercury and Venus IC lines just outside Johannesburg, but more importantly, also crossing the Zambezi River at the point where we started our life together in that tent. The Moon MC line runs through the Western Cape, where Jan and I had a wonderful holiday, while the Uranus rise line crosses the Mercury/Venus conjunction close to Johannesburg. The Sun/Uranus Paran runs right through the northern suburbs of Johannesburg, exactly where Jan was driving home that night, and where I held the fateful seminar.

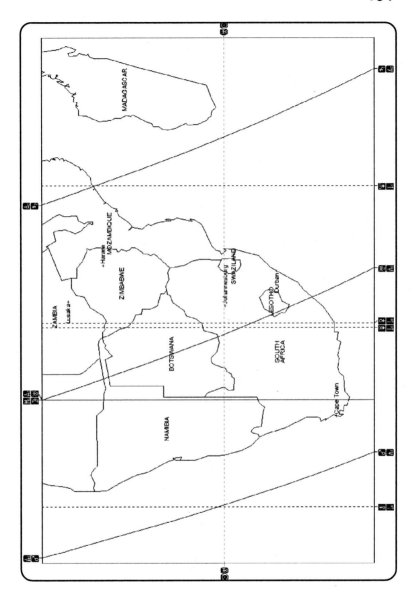

Sasha Fenton - Astro-Map chart

Appendix

Where To Obtain Maps, Reports, Programs and All Other Forms of Astrological Information

There is a very good directory called "Astrology; The Yearbook of Worldwide Astrology", which comes out every year and which costs around £5 ($7), plus whatever extra is needed for postage and packing. This contains information on groups, organizations, software suppliers, shops, events and just about everything else that is going on, or that is obtainable, all over the world. Contact the Midheaven Bookshop website mentioned below. You will probably be able to find software companies that are local to your part of the world in this Yearbook.

Equinox supplies charts, reports, books and much more. The Astrology Shop in London is linked with Equinox, and these website addresses are www.equinox.uk.com and www.astrology.co.uk. Nowadays, the most consistent addresses are websites - phones and other details change too frequently to be relied upon in a book like this one. Equinox also operates from Australia, the USA, and elsewhere through agencies.

The Midheaven Bookshop in London supplies books, software and much else, and the website is located at www.midheavenbooks.com

For up-to-date information on a vast range of astrological software, visit www.microcycles.com. Some software houses have arrangements where you can try before you buy; so look around, try things out and see for yourself whether you want something simple or complex, and whether you simply want calculation and charting software, or something that will give you a printed report.

Solar Fire software, including Solar Maps, is obtainable in the UK from Roy Gillett Consultants, 32 Glynswood, Camberley, Surrey GU15 1HU. Roy's email address is roy.gillett@dial.pipex.com. The Solar Fire range is also available in the USA, from Astrolabe at www.alabe.com The nice thing about Solar Maps is that it has quite a useful report program built in at no extra cost.

Look for products under the Winstar label, which are obtainable from Matrix USA and UK. Matrix supplies a range of software, from the most comprehensive to some really useful and relatively inexpensive items. Contact Martin Davis of Matrix UK at: www.matrixastrology.com; his email address is: martin@matrixastrology.com

Matrix is an American company that advertises in all good astrology publications and they can also be found on the Internet, via the above website.

An excellent American astrology magazine that has fascinating articles and useful advertisements for all kinds of products is called The Mountain Astrologer. Its website is www.mountainastrologer.com

An excellent quarterly UK Magazine is Astrolore, which you can find on the Internet at www.astrolore.co.uk.

Suggested Reading List

Many of the ideas on this list were kindly given to me by Ariel Guttman. I do not have full details of publishers or the dates of publication for all the books listed, but that is not a problem any longer, if you visit an Internet bookshop such as Amazon.com or Amazon.co.uk. If you have difficulty in obtaining any of these books through an Internet bookshop, try contacting the Astrology Shop in London through their website at www.astrologyshop.co.uk.

Astrolocality Astrology by Martin Davis
Where in the World with Astro*Carto*Graphy by David Meadows
Mundane Astrology by Baigent, Campion and Harvey.
The Book of World Horoscopes by Nicholas Campion.
Planets in Locality by Steve Cozzi (Llewellyn 1986).
Working With Local Space by Zipporah Dobyns.
Horoscopes of US Cities and States by Carolyn Dodson.
Various articles on Local Space by Michael Erlewine.
Earth Astrology by Ariel Guttman.
Navigating by the Stars by Edith Hathaway.
Working With Astrology by Michael Harding and Charles Harvey.
The Astro*Carto*Graphy Book of Maps by Jim Lewis and Ariel Guttman.
The Astrology of Macrocosm edited by Joan McEvers.
The Geodetic World Map by Chris McRae.
The Book of World Horoscopes by Moon Moore.

Horoscopes of the Western Hemisphere by Marc Penfield.
Astrological Timing by Dane Rudhyar.
Geodetic Equivalents by Sepharial.
Planets on the Move by Maritha Pottenger and Zipporah
    Dobyns. (ACS 1995)
The Psychology of Astro*Carto*Graphy by Kenneth Irving
    and Jim Lewis (Arkana 1997).

Index

Chinese Divinations

Sasha Fenton

"A unique Compendium of Chinese Divinations..."

Sasha Fenton wanted to see if it is possible to produce
one book, containing the basics of many different Chinese
Divinations - and she more than achieved her aim!

This book goes much further than just the basics, and proves that
Westerners can understand Chinese systems with ease.

~~~~~

Contents include:

Face Reading	Feng Shui
Mah Jong Reading	Chinese Hand Reading
The Four Pillars of Destiny	Nine Star Ki (The Lo Shu)
Weighing the Bones	Yarrow Stick Reading

and a Chinese Lunar Oracle.

Paperback	ISBN 0-9533478-5-0
240 pages	£9.99

Star*Date*Oracle

Sasha Fenton & Jonathan Dee
"Ancient Lore for Today's World..."

Got a Problem?
Need a quick decision?
Choose the right day for:
~ Getting or starting a job
~ That hot date
~ Travel & holiday planning
~ Fixing things at home
or planning anything else...

The *Star*Date*Oracle*
highlights your best timing,
for any hour, any day, any year!

~~~~~

And there's More!
The *List of Fates*
reveals the destiny in the name you use every day -
not necessarily your birth name,
or an unloved "official" name;

~~~~~

Finally, the *Mystic Pyramid*
unleashes your own intuition
helped by your Guardian Angel,
and gives instant answers to
your most pressing problems.

~~~~~

*The sources are ancient, but the results are
right up-to-date, easy to understand and easy to use!*

Paperback   ISBN 1-903065-15-1
150 pages   £5.99

Prophecy for Profit

Sasha Fenton & Jan Budkowski
"The essential Career & Business Guide for those who give Readings"

Sasha Fenton and her husband Jan Budkowski combine decades of divinatory & financial skills in this internationally oriented book.

<u>Subjects covered include:</u>
Organisational methods ~ A mental & physical health guide ~ Starting-up costs ~ Building up your clientele ~ Managing finance & cashflow ~ Working in fairs & festivals ~ The Marine Bandsman Syndrome ~ Psychic protection ~ Teaching & Lecturing ~ and much more!

~~~~~

If you're serious about your career, this is the book for you - whatever your interests, from Astrology to Zoomancy!

~~~~~

"This book is a true gemstone. It should be on every Reader's MUST HAVE list, and should be recommended to anyone working part time or professionally, or indeed considering Reading as a vocation."
Andrew Smith, The Celtic Astrologer magazine

Paperback   ISBN 0-9533478-1-8
240 pages   £10.95

Fortune Telling by Tarot Cards

Sasha Fenton
"A Beginner's Guide to Understanding the Tarot"

This invaluable book has sold over 500,000 copies worldwide,
confirming that Sasha's well-known, friendly & accessible style clearly
sets a standard amongst the multitude of Tarot books available today.

Fully revised, updated and packed with fresh information for today's
world, Sasha's popular title is once again available.
Now illustrated throughout, with the new Jonathan Dee Tarot deck!

This book is the ideal introduction to the Tarot!

Contents include:

Tarot origins ~ Intro to Major & Minor Arcana
Clear card interpretations ~ Linked / Synthesized card Readings
Simple, Complex & Special Purpose Readings
Volunteer Readings - and what happened later!

Paperback
216 pages

ISBN 1-903065-18-6
£9.99

ASTRO*CARTO*GRAPHY® Maps & Analyses

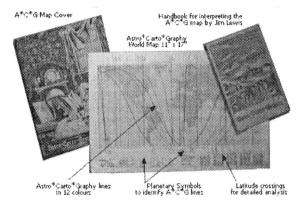

A*C*G Map Cover

Handbook for interpreting the A*C*G map by Jim Lewis

Astro*Carto*Graphy World Map 11" x 17"

Astro*Carto*Graphy lines in 12 colours

Planetary Symbols to identify A*C*G lines

Latitude crossings for detailed analysis

Astro*Carto*Graphy by Jim Lewis

Start your journey of self-discovery with your Astro*Carto*Graphy map.

Our maps were designed and authorised by the late Jim Lewis, founder and pioneer of A*C*G. Jim devoted his life to research, writing, teaching and lecturing on A*C*G.

Astro*Carto*Graphy Map Kit: £18/$24

The Map Kit consists of a World Map (with cities and borders) plus a 44 page interpretive handbook by Jim Lewis. The 49 A*C*G lines, which include Chiron and the Node lines, are set out in 12 colours, with symbols for ease of identification.

Map Kit plus 3 location analysis:
combined price: **£34/$40**
Analysis for 3 locations: £20/US$30

Postage: Please add £1.50/US$2.50 per order (no matter how many items) for post & packing to any location worldwide.

In addition, you can order an individual report (approximately 10,000 words) describing the astrological influences on you in any 3 locations around the world. Using **Jim Lewis's** text base, your **3 City Analysis** explores the psychological and practical conditions you're likely to encounter.

Locations must be towns or cities (rather than countries) and they need to be at least 300 miles apart.

To receive your map or analysis within 10 working days, we require your date, time and place of birth, address & 3 locations.

*   www.astrology.co.uk

*   **Email:** equinox@equinox.uk.com

*   Visit Equinox at the Astrology Shop, 78 Neal St. London WC2

*   **UK Tel:** 01624 827000 Fax: 827 876

*   **USA:** Tel/Fax: 503 296 2069

*   **Australia:** Tel/Fax: +61 (2) 9475 0175

*   **Write to:** Equinox Astrology, The Mill House, Santon, Isle of Man, IM4 1EX

ORDER FORM

Order via our website, or send this form & payment to:
Zambezi Publishing Ltd, P.O. Box 221, Plymouth, Devn
PL2 2YJ (UK)
N.B: Please check up-to-date prices on our website first
Please send me the following book(s):

TITLE	PRICE	No.	TOTAL
_____	£ _____	// ____	£ _____
_____	£ _____	// ____	£ _____
_____	£ _____	// ____	£ _____
_____	£ _____	// ____	£ _____
P & P:			£ _____
TOTAL:			**£** _____

(block capitals, please):
Name:_____
Address: _____
_____
_____
Zip: _____ Country: _____
Tel : _____ Fax: _____
e-mail:_____

Signature: _____

P & P (UK): £1.50 for one book, add £1.00 per book.
O'seas orders: 1 book: P&P £4.50, then £1.50 per bk.

Payment (UK): Cheque, cash, postal orders.
Elsewhere: Br £ or EURO international money orders; easiest of
all, order via a UK / USA internet bookshop, or direct from our website
(www.zampub.com)

Printed in the United Kingdom
by Lightning Source UK Ltd.
109964UKS00001B/139-168